CEN 09/05

 Geordan Murphy
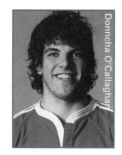 Donncha O'Callaghan
 Paul O'Connell
 Ronan O'Gara
 Malcolm O'Kelly

 Michael Owen
 Dwayne Peel
 Jason Robinson
 Graham Rowntree
 Tom Shanklin

 Andrew Sheridan
 Steve Thompson

 Andy Titterell
 Shane Williams

 Brent Cockbain
 Simon Easterby
 Ryan Jones
 Simon Shaw
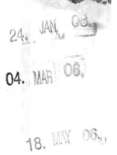 Jason White

24. JAN 06.
04. MAR 06.
18. MAY 06.

D0548615

6 384 545 000

Copying recordings is illegal. All recorded items
are hired entirely at hirer's own risk

THE INSIDE STORY OF THE
LIONS IN NEW ZEALAND 2005

Blacked Out

Mick Cleary

Edited by
IAN ROBERTSON

with contributions from
**Brendan Gallagher,
Alastair Hignell and Terry Cooper**

Photographs by
Getty Images and Fotosport UK

MAINSTREAM
PUBLISHING

Copyright © Lennard Associates Limited 2005

First published in Great Britain in 2005 by
MAINSTREAM PUBLISHING COMPANY (EDINBURGH) LTD
7 Albany Street
Edinburgh EH1 3UG

ISBN 1 84596 059 9

A catalogue record for this book is available from the British Library

Produced by Lennard Books
A division of Lennard Associates Limited
Mackerye End, Harpenden, Herts, AL5 5DR

Production Editor: Chris Marshall
Text and cover design: Paul Cooper Design

Printed and bound in Great Britain by
Bath Press

Contents

Real Pubs, Real Beer,
Real Passion!

17 99

GREENE KING

www.greeneking.co.uk

Foreword by David Elliott

Managing Director, Greene King Pub Partners

The very fact that the British & Irish Lions only tour New Zealand once every twelve years makes such a trip very special. In the previous sixteen years the Lions had enjoyed two wonderfully successful tours to Australia in 1989 and South Africa in 1997, winning the series on each occasion by two Tests to one.

In one hundred years of rugby they have only ever won a Test series in New Zealand once. That was in 1971 when they went into the fourth and final Test leading two Tests to one and drew that final match to clinch an historic moment.

That shows just how hard it is to win in New Zealand. The 2005 Lions gave it their best shot but they came up against an exceptionally good All Blacks team.

Greene King are delighted and proud to sponsor this book. Rugby tours and beer go rather well together and the 20,000 Lions supporters who swept through the Land of the Long White Cloud had six weeks to savour delicacies such as the Greene King special brew – Old Speckled Hen. The supporters had a ball from start to finish. Every street in every city was a sea of red jerseys. The spirit was fantastic.

In the UK Greene King is heavily involved in rugby, being on tap in over 500 rugby clubs in England alone. We were thrilled with the efforts of our club with the highest profile – Wasps – when they won the Premiership final in May.

We are really pleased to throw our weight behind rugby and it was a natural extension to support the 2005 Lions. The magnificent performance by the All Blacks in the second Test in Wellington will live in the memory for a long time to come.

The Test series may have been lost but the Lions remain the most famous brand in rugby. The heroic victories of 1971, 1974, 1989 and 1997 were no flash in the pan. Let's raise a glass to the Lions in South Africa in 2009.

BELOW On tour with the Lions – David Elliott (centre in Lions shirt) on the eve of the final Test with members of the BBC commentary team: (left to right) Ian Robertson, Jason Leonard, Jill Douglas, Alastair Hignell and Eric Peters.

JVC DVD Compact Component System

DVD - Audio high-quality sound playback.
Hybrid Feedback Digital Amplifier for
superior high-fidelity virtual sound.
30 watts x 2 RMS.
AM/FM tuner. Beautiful natural sound.

Sources: DVD-Audio/Video, DVD-R/-RW(Video Format), CD, SVCD/VCD, CD-R/RW, MP3/JPEG (CD-R/RW), Tuner • Power Output: 30W x 2 (RMS)
8cm Full-Range Wood Cone Speakers • Display Dimmer • COMPU PLAY • Sleep Timer • Electronic Bass/Treble Tone Controls • RDS Tuner with Enhanced
Other Network • Programme (99 tracks) / Random / Repeat Play • Original Birch Wood Cone Speaker for natural resonance with ideal acoustic characteristics
DVD-Audio high-quality sound playback • Hybrid Feedback Digital Amplifier for noiseless, high-fidelity sound • Dolby Digital/DTS Decoder (2ch) • DVD Express
Play Start • 192kHz/24-bit Audio D/A Converter • 10-bit/54MHz Video D/A Converter • Virtual Surround • Die-cast aluminium speaker frame and edgewise-wound
4-layer voice coil for a dynamic sound • 21-pin SCART Out • Screw-type Gold-plated Speaker Terminals • Independent Power Supply

EX-P1 DVD COMPACT COMPONENT SYSTEM

World's First Wood Cone Speakers

WOOD CONE

WOOD CONE

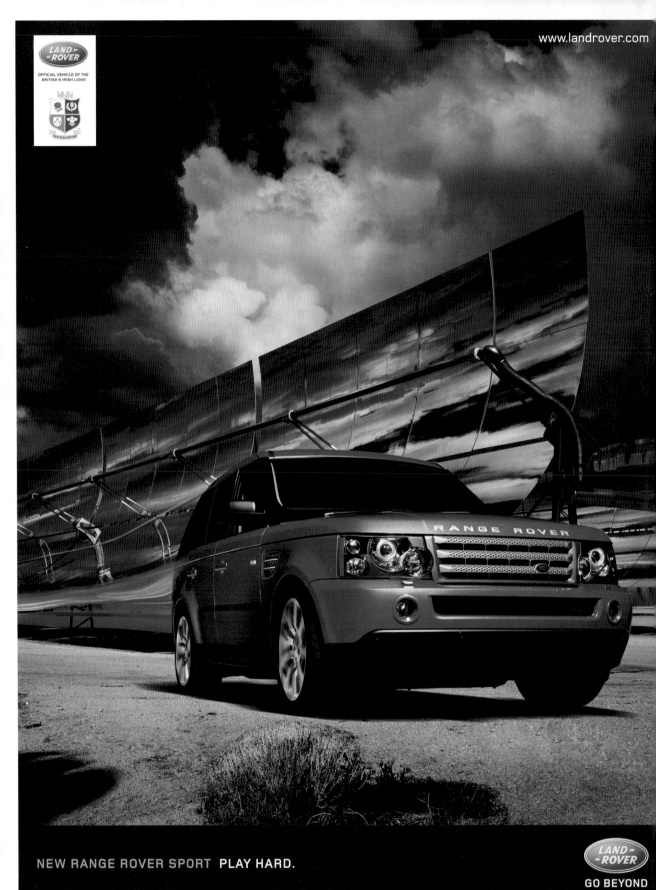

1

In the Beginning

'Alastair Campbell?! You must be joking.' He wasn't. Sir Clive Woodward doesn't do gags. Well, not when it comes to the day job. He had hired the country's most famed spin doctor to head up the press operation in New Zealand. Campbell was a vanity appointment by Woodward. Nothing wrong with that. He wanted the best. And that's what he hired – a former hack with the sharpest, if occasionally the most poisonous, pen in the Street.

No one could take issue with Campbell's credentials. He knew the trade well. Perhaps too well. There is little need to finesse evident truths in rugby in quite the way that reality is stood on its head on a daily basis in politics. The smoke and mirrors world of Westminster is a far cry from the muck and bullets beat of the rugby writer.

There were many who found issue with Campbell being brought into the Lions fold. It didn't bother me in the slightest. There was a

concern over his contractual columns that were to be done for *The Times*, but shots were duly fired across the bows on that one. Campbell knew where the line was. You might argue that his presence was over the top, an unnecessary addition to the already swollen ranks of back-up staff. Lions chief executive John Feehan is a considerable man. Those broad shoulders, honed in the dark front-row recesses for Old Belvedere, Old Wesley and Leinster among others, had grown used to bearing the strain of

2 July 2004: Sir Clive Woodward, Bill Beaumont and Lions chief executive John Feehan face the media at London's Roehampton Club.

Woodward's ever-expanding squad. Another day, another dollar – that was Feehan's lot. Woodward wanted Campbell. Woodward got Campbell.

Once the committee of the British and Irish Lions decided that Woodward was the man to head up the 2005 tour, they knew what they were letting themselves in for. They knew Woodward would deliver. He could not guarantee success on the field. Sport bends the knee to no deity, let alone human, when it comes to preordaining results. What Woodward could guarantee, though, was that his squad would be in the best possible physical and mental state to take on the All Blacks. Woodward was a winner. The players would know that. And, more importantly, the New Zealanders would know it.

Every single time the All Blacks had set foot in the British Isles there had been a rush to describe the aura that surrounded them. The black shirt, the silver fern, the haka – the mythology was powerful and all-consuming. Many opponents were beaten before they set foot on the field. That mystique had been eroded. Woodward's England stripped away several layers when winning against the odds in Wellington prior to the 2003 World Cup. The All Blacks had also peeled away a few coatings themselves by underperforming in the previous two World Cups at least; four World Cups if you are being very harsh. Let's be harsh. The All Blacks are not all they are cracked up to be. A proud country with a wonderful rugby tradition. But unbeatable? Look at the statistics not the myth. Woodward did. 'We respect them but we do not fear them,' said Woodward as his men prepared to fly south. Lose the mind games and you've lost the plot.

This then was the Lions asserting their own identity. The Kiwis knew what Woodward had done with England. They may not have liked it. But they would respect it. They knew that the Lions would arrive in good shape. They would want for nothing. They would cover all bases. And, therefore, they would be formidable opponents. That's what Woodward's appointment meant.

History was against the Lions. They had only one series victory to their name in over a century of trying. Carwyn James's side had done it in 1971 through the sheer brilliance of its coach and the

outrageous talent of its players. There were a few tough hombres in the mix as well. Such moments do not pass by very often, such symmetry of genius and ruggedness – rugby's perfect cocktail.

Woodward was the obvious choice as head coach. It took only a couple of months following England's World Cup victory in Australia for the committee to rubber-stamp his appointment. Ireland's Eddie O'Sullivan was also theoretically in the running, but fine coach as he is, the Irishman simply could not match Woodward's CV. Who could in these parts? There was no mistaking the entry from 22 November 2003: England 20 Australia 17. Game, set, match, trophy and exultant celebrations across the land.

Woodward was viewed – probably still is viewed – with a certain suspicion. Too headstrong. Too outspoken. Too gimmicky. The conservative world of English rugby was given a shake-up by

Woodward's arrival. He doesn't have much time for convention. Or not convention for convention's sake. If it needs changing then he will change it. Woodward does have an eye for certain traditions. He is a passionate Englishman, one who has always had an admiration for Australians and their brashness and brazenness about all things 'ocker'. Woodward sees nothing wrong in being proud of one's country.

Would his Englishness count against him? Was he too overtly red rose in the eyes of the Celts? It's fair to say that Woodward's picture was probably not pinned to the bedroom walls of too many fans in those countries – the archetypal Englishman with his money and his fancy ways.

But cut through the cliché and a wholly different picture emerges. You can't bluff your way to a World Cup. You don't get lucky for six weeks in succession. You don't fluke 12 successive wins over the southern hemisphere Big Three – New Zealand, Australia and South Africa. Woodward had backed his bold talk with commendable deeds. And he had done that by hard work and smart thinking. No detail was overlooked. No method was thought to be out of bounds; no approach too unlikely or unworthy. Some things were ditched. Others were taken on board. One of the first things Woodward did on taking over as England coach in 1997 was to head down to Harley Street in London to find the best nutritionist in the marketplace. The deal was done in double-quick time. In the committee rooms of Twickenham, eyebrows soared. Too late. Woodward was on the move. It was his way or no way. It's now the norm for every last calorie to be accounted for, every last legal supplement to be popped. Stand still in professional sport and you go backwards. Woodward realised that pretty damn quickly.

For nutritionist on this trip read Campbell – Dave Campbell, that is. The Lions took a travelling chef with them, the same man who had accompanied England wherever they had gone for the past few years. Dave Campbell is a Scot but came into contact with the England rugby team at Pennyhill Park in Bagshot, the five-star country house hotel that England adopted as their base in the wake of the 1999 Rugby World Cup. Campbells, the pair of them (no relation), the best there was – that was the Woodward imprimatur, the stamp of quality. 'We want to do 100 things one per cent better than anybody else' is a phrase that Woodward has often used. What worked so spectacularly for England was now to be applied to the Lions.

Woodward had been in Australia in 2001 when the Lions fell at the final hurdle against the Wallabies. That side ought to have seen off Australia. They had by far the better pack at their disposal, led by Martin Johnson with able lieutenants alongside in Keith Wood, Richard Hill, Neil Back and Phil Vickery. They had match winners behind the scrum in Brian O'Driscoll and Jason Robinson. And they had the boot of Jonny Wilkinson, although the England fly half was below par with his goal-kicking on that tour.

As the many thousands of Lions supporters who thronged Brisbane for that sensational first Test will tell you, the combo of O'Driscoll and Robinson cut the Wallaby defence to shreds. The refrain of 'Waltzing O'Driscoll' rang round the Gabba that night as the young Ireland centre left Wallabies on their backsides as he wove past them en route to the try line. And yet the Lions lost the series. True, they were only undone by a last-ditch line-out steal from Justin Harrison over Johnson, but they lost. Memories fade. Record books do not. It doesn't matter one jot that the Lions came so close to glory. They lost. Period.

Woodward studied that tour from close quarters. He saw the failings. Well, it didn't take much to spot them. Scrum half Matt Dawson exposed many of them in his diary published in *The Daily Telegraph*. Dawson was slated for not keeping his thoughts to himself. The truth would have come out one way or another. And it was as well that it did. The Lions camp was not a happy one. And certainly not for those who did not fit the bill in Graham Henry's eyes. The New Zealand-born Wales coach, in opposition to Woodward for the 2005 trip as All Black coach, had made an early call on the 2001 tour, relegating his midweek side to the status of also-rans by publicly declaring that the Test team was all that mattered. It was a PR gaffe, even if the sentiments behind it were understandable.

Lions tours are tricky balancing acts. There is not enough time to really fine-tune a side that might cope with the organisation and togetherness of a Test opponent. That has been the same down the generations. In the modern era, it has even more relevance. Professional Test sides spend months in camp, honing their systems in defence and attack.

Henry went for route one. He dumped on the dirt-trackers and he flogged his main men. The players were tired and they were unhappy. Henry was also unlucky in that injury struck. In the final training session prior to the decisive third Test in Sydney, Henry had only eight fit players at his disposal. Woodward listened and learnt.

By the summer of 2004 he had already done significant work, unveiling his plans at a press conference one July morning in Roehampton, southwest London. Woodward was to be a guest of the All England Lawn Tennis Club at Wimbledon that afternoon. He played a few flashing verbal volleys himself that morning. He was not going to be derailed by unforeseen injuries. Woodward announced that he was going to take the biggest ever Lions squad of players for the 11-match trip (the Auckland game had yet to be confirmed at that point). He had a total of 44 players in mind. As it turned out, some bloke by the name of Wilkinson managed to sneak in through the back door to increase the numbers by one.

Woodward's master stroke was to reveal that he was going to have two coaching teams, who would dedicate themselves to ensuring that each team, be it midweek or Saturday side, would have full and proper preparation. The Lions head coach played down fears that he was intent on splitting the party into two distinct teams. 'There is no way that you can dissect a tour party into two separate groups,' he said. 'Every player will have a fundamental chance to play in the Test team. But there will be two coaching teams: one to prepare the midweek side and the other the Saturday or Test side. That allows each group to be prepared properly. We sent arguably our strongest ever party to Australia and played against one of the weakest Wallaby teams and yet we lost. Everyone came back absolutely shattered. Ben Cohen [the England wing] said that he'd never go on a Lions tour again and that was a quote I thought I'd never hear. The manager's report recommended fewer matches and fewer players for future Lions tours. I disagree. There should be more matches and more players. It's not an exact science but every player should start at least three matches and play no more than six.'

His message was clearly expressed. But that didn't stop him being quizzed many times over the coming months as to why he was splitting the Test players from the midweek side. Perhaps he should have had Alastair Campbell on board then to spell it out. The coaches would be split; the players would not. There was to be a gangway between the teams. All a player asks for is a fair break. He wants to show what he can do. That's all. Woodward was determined to give them all a crack at it. As he was to point out on the eve of departure. 'I will be picking on form not on reputation,' said Woodward. 'Like everyone, I have got an idea of a Test side in my head. But I also have a very clear idea of what Lions tours are about. People always do come through very strongly. When these players do get a chance, they have got to step up to the mark.'

Clear enough. Intriguingly at that July conference, Woodward dangled the tantalising possibility that even those who had retired from international rugby might be considered. The names of Wales scrum half Rob Howley, Scotland's Bryan Redpath, Wales No. 8 Scott Quinnell and even Martin Johnson were tossed Woodward's way.

'Well, there's a couple of names there I'd love to see available,' he said with a smile.

As it turned out, within a couple of months Woodward himself had retired from front-line international duties, so too his last England captain, Lawrence Dallaglio. They both still made the trip, as did Neil Back. No Johnson, though. He made the right call. His time was up. He would never have considered retiring just to preserve his reputation. However, for the rest of us, the image of him holding aloft the Webb Ellis Cup was seared into the memory as his last act on an international rugby field. Johnson spared us the punch-drunk boxer's routine of going one round too far.

Woodward's shock resignation from the England job in September 2004 was great news for the Lions. It meant that he would be able to dedicate himself wholeheartedly to the Lions cause. Henry was to admit that he perhaps ought not to have taken on the Lions role in 2001 when he was still in charge of the national side in Wales. It was too onerous a burden, and indeed was to cause rifts within Welsh rugby that were not to heal. Eight months later Henry headed home to New Zealand, that benighted tour to Australia still dogging him.

From 1 September Woodward could declare himself to be a neutral. He was no longer an Englishman doubling as Lions coach. He was the British and Irish Lions head coach, above all perceived bias and favouritism. He didn't waste the opportunity. Woodward spent time in all three Celtic camps – Wales first as they prepared to face New Zealand in the November Test, then Scotland and Ireland. He also had time with both Italy and France as they went through their paces prior to taking on the All Blacks.

Woodward was not short of information, both on his own potential players as well as on the opposition. It was time well spent. Woodward did overcome many of the suspicions, did build bridges with all the Home Union countries. The players got a sense of him, too; how he is and how he operates. Fair play, too, to the respective coaches. Given that Woodward was so closely associated with England, it was a big call to allow him to see what happens behind the scenes.

ABOVE Self-assured and assured of his place – Ireland skipper and 2005 Lions captain Brian O'Driscoll pictured at the Lions team announcement event at the Hilton, Heathrow, on 11 April 2005.

Woodward was equally even-handed in compiling his coaching team. No favours, no elevating old mates above others. He ended up with a cast list fit for any production. Ian McGeechan, the most successful coach in Lions history with wins in Australia (1989) and South Africa (1997) as well as honourable defeat in New Zealand in 1993, was drafted in to head up the midweek coaching panel. McGeechan would have Llanelli's Gareth Jenkins and Ireland defence coach Mike Ford to assist. Eddie O'Sullivan would work alongside Andy Robinson and Phil Larder with the Saturday team. Kicking guru Dave Alred would operate with both groups.

By the time the plane departed Heathrow on 25 May, Woodward had fleshed out the management team with several other notable names. Dave Reddin, England's much-acclaimed fitness adviser, was teamed with Craig White, who had done great things with Ireland and then Wasps on the conditioning front. Dr James Robson led the medical team, bringing the wisdom accumulated over three previous Lions tours. Robson was a good practitioner and a popular man, one able to work on the mind as well as the body. The players all knew he had their best interests at heart. Gary O'Driscoll, who worked with Ireland, was to assist.

The physiotherapy team, who put in more hours on tours than any other group (except, of course, journalists, who have to stay up into the wee small hours purely in the interests of nocturnal research – their dedication knows no bounds), contained the familiar figures of Phil Pask, Richard Wegrzyk, Bob Stewart and Stuart Barton. Video analysis was in the capable hands of Tony Biscombe and Gavin Scott. The back-up staff also included the kit men, Dave Tennison and Dave Pearson; and the media assistants, Ben Wilson, Marcus Jansa and Louisa Cheetham.

Former international referee David McHugh was along to keep everyone onside, while in a legal sense the same could be said of Richard Smith QC, whose first job was to try and get the suspension of Leicester flanker Neil Back down to the bare minimum. Back was cited after belting Joe Worsley in the Premiership final only a few days before the squad congregated at their Vale of Glamorgan base.

Smith argued for a one-match ban; Back got four weeks, thereby ruling him out of the opening four games, including the match against Argentina at the Millennium Stadium. Woodward declared at one point that 'Neil thinks he is innocent', one of the more improbable statements in recent times given that Back was caught on camera swinging his right fist into the face of Worsley, who slumped to the ground and then needed 13 stitches in a nasty mouth wound. Yes, but apart from that, just why might you think him guilty?

One of the key cogs to keep it all whirring was Louise Ramsay, the team manager, the one who had studiously compiled dossiers on every logistical eventuality. It couldn't have worked without her input. The tour manager, Bill Beaumont, was an old-school operator, a much-respected figure round the world, just the man to keep the Kiwis at bay.

So much for the back-room staff. They laboured for love, and a few quid, and were happy to stay away from the limelight. The whole shebang was to cost the fat end of £10 million.

Of more interest to the outside world was the composition of the squad itself. Woodward first had to decide on his captain. Ireland's Brian O'Driscoll was the one strong runner, although there were a few speculative punts on Munster lock Paul O'Connell – wild assumptions if truth be known, given that O'Connell, a decent fellow and good second-row forward, still had to press his claim for inclusion in the squad let alone the Test side.

You could have made a good case for Lawrence Dallaglio, a man who has never known where the reverse gear is located on a rugby field. Dallaglio was Woodward's initial choice as England captain way back when, and even if that relationship had cooled over the years, there was still enormous respect for what the Wasps man had to offer. Woodward had suggested that it would take monumental persuasion for him to look for players outside those taking part in the Six Nations. He said one thing but meant another. Dallaglio's name was always in mind. Stern, unforgiving, relentlessly upbeat, Dallaglio had few equals in world rugby when it came to facing down a challenge. It was too big a call, though, to venture outside the international grouping for the captain.

O'Driscoll was the man for the job, revealed by Woodward when the squad was finally unveiled at a glitzy gathering at Heathrow Airport and broadcast live on BSkyB. The Ireland centre was a good choice. The reasoning was simple. O'Driscoll was one of the very few men assured of his place in the Test side. Respect is not easily won within changing rooms. Other players can sniff a phoney from 20 paces. O'Driscoll had no case to plead for being part of any Test side in the world. His name was already inked in. His team-mates knew that. So too the opposition.

There was more. O'Driscoll, articulate, media-savvy and no shrinking violet out where it hurts on the field, had other qualities. Popular bloke as he was among his peers, he was no cardboard cut-out Paddy, full of bonhomie and easy charm. Those stereotypes are misleading if not downright worthless. O'Driscoll knows his own mind. He is shrewd and he is sharp. He is not afraid to say what he thinks – just the type you need when dealing with Woodward.

Woodward admits himself that he doesn't want to be surrounded by yes-men. He wants his ideas to be challenged. He wants to be told when to back off. Johnson did that during the World Cup, as did other senior players following that fright against Wales in the quarter-final. They needed more rest. Woodward was left in no doubt about that. The players got what they wanted. O'Driscoll is cut from the same stone. Not that he would ape Johnson. That would be a sham. Johnson was Johnson – all glower, all stony intent, but also an intelligent reader of the game.

O'Driscoll was informed that he was to be captain a fortnight before Woodward went public with his squad. 'This will be without doubt the most intense rugby challenge of my life,' said Ireland's captain. There was to be no doubting that.

He had plenty of good men alongside him in the trenches. Fourteen of England's 2003 World Cup squad were on board, including scrum half Matt Dawson, who got the nod instead of Leicester's Harry Ellis, who had started ahead of him for England. England provided 20 players in the initial squad announced, ahead of Ireland with 11, Wales ten and Scotland just three. Back and Dallaglio, both of whom had retired from international rugby, were chosen, with the 36-year-old Leicester flanker becoming the oldest Lion since Wales prop Charlie Faulkner in 1977. There were gripes that Grand Slam Wales ought to have had a larger representation. Nip and tuck calls on the fringes have to go one way or t'other. Woodward went with those he knew – the Greenwoods, the Hills – and took wise counsel on the value of the Sale front-row pairing, for example: hooker Andy Titterrell and prop Andrew Sheridan.

The players were to be informed of their selection by the wonders of modern technology – text message. Quicker than first-class post but no more reliable. Only about a dozen or so of the squad duly got the cheering beep-beep of the text message at the appropriate time. Others just had to sweat it out, fearing the worst. Ireland centre Gordon D'Arcy couldn't stand the tension so put his mobile to one side. Shortly after midday a pal phoned to say that his name was not among those released on the Lions website. D'Arcy's heart sank only to soar again a few minutes later as Beaumont called out his name at the live TV broadcast. There were other such dramas played out across the four countries. The cock-up was quite endearing and added to the theatricality of the occasion. It occurred because one player had supplied the wrong mobile number, throwing the others out of kilter. The lines of communication would need to be better oiled when it came to the real thing.

Beaumont read through the names – Back, Balshaw (who was forced to withdraw through injury as the squad congregated in Wales eight days before departure), Bulloch, Byrne … On and on went the list until the last few end-of-alphabet names appeared – White, Williams (Martyn), Williams (Shane). And that was that.

No Jonny Wilkinson. Had England's Golden Boy not passed muster? Was it too late for him to prove that he was fit? The trauma of injury had stalked Wilkinson since that night of glory in Sydney. He was approaching his fourth comeback, his serious neck problem having given way to biceps and then knee injuries through the season. Wilkinson had played so little rugby. No one quite knew if his body could hold out for real. No one, that is, except Wilkinson, who stated that he felt ready and raring to go. Woodward declared that he would be added if he could prove himself fit. To Woodward and to the others in the group. It was an intriguing call by the head coach. There is usually a sting in the tail when Woodward is around.

Two of Wilkinson's World Cup team-mates were also raging against the dying of the Lions light. Prop Phil Vickery and centre Mike Tindall, ailing with arm and foot injuries respectively, were also cut some slack by Woodward, but their cause looked forlorn. 'The chances for those two, though, are very remote,' said Woodward. 'The clock is against them while it is not necessarily so against Jonny.' So it proved.

Woodward took pains to emphasise that he did not want to be seen to be favouring Wilkinson above other players, several of whom had had to struggle through injury. Wales flanker Colin Charvis, a clubmate of Wilkinson, had just returned to action after missing the Six Nations Championship but did not make the squad. England's World Cup duo of centre Will Greenwood and back-row Richard Hill, both of whom had played their first games the preceding weekend, did win call-ups.

Woodward made a point of calling the three other fly halves in the party – Stephen Jones, Ronan O'Gara and Charlie Hodgson – the night before the announcement to outline his proposal for Wilkinson. He was especially keen to impress on Jones, who had an outstanding campaign for Grand Slam-winning Wales, that even if Wilkinson were to come through, his place in the Test team was no formality. A sense of harmony is basic to the success of any Lions tour. It was not enough that Wilkinson should merely be on a rugby field over the coming weeks. He had to be on form, too.

'If Jonny comes through the next few games for his club and is looking at his best, then he will be added to the squad,' said Woodward. 'If he does make it, then fine. But he'll face a hell of a fight for the Test spot. It would be wrong at this stage to pick a player for the Lions squad that clearly has not got through 80 minutes of rugby for a long, long time. But Jonny is an exceptional player, one of the mentally toughest characters I've ever come across. We all know how much he wants to play, how much Lions supporters and the New Zealand public want to see him play, and this is the best way of keeping this prospect alive. The other fly halves fully support my decision.' Well, they would, wouldn't they? No point bad-mouthing the boss too early in the trip.

Wilkinson made it, his selection confirmed just a couple of hours after he played a full part in Newcastle's game at Gloucester in early May.

Feehan was forced to do some more sums – player number 45 was on board. 'If there was any light at the end of the tunnel as I waited for the scan on my second knee injury, then it was not a very bright one,' said Wilkinson. 'I enjoyed being backed into a corner like that. I'd rather be fighting for my place than be given it because of reputation. There was pressure there for me to stake my claim. I had to work tooth and nail for it and although that made me very nervous, that's a good sign. I don't want to live off my laurels. You have to earn the right to play. I hated that feeling of not being able to get the respect of other players by not being able to get out there. So, I'm very lucky to be here, grateful too.'

The squad was originally announced on 11 April. There was still a lot of rugby to be played between then and departure. Time for dark thoughts to gather. Time for fate to pick its victim and deal out its sinister hand. Only one man was to be felled from above – Leeds full back Iain Balshaw, who was to pay dearly for his decision to contest the Powergen Cup final for his club when not fully fit. His subsequent quad muscle injury was to rule him out. One man's misfortune is another's opportunity. Woodward wasted no time in summoning England wing Mark Cueto, by universal consent the player considered the most unlucky of all to miss out originally. Even Woodward seemed to think so as he greeted a shell-shocked Cueto into camp. The Sale wing, the most productive in the country with 27 tries in 33 games, thought it was a cruel wind-up when he was called from the training pitch in Stockport that morning as the club went through their final preparation for the upcoming European Challenge Cup final against Pau. Cueto had watched four team-mates – Jason Robinson, Andrew Sheridan, Andy Titterrell and Charlie Hodgson – leave ten minutes earlier to head down the motorway to spend a day with the Lions before being released to finish their club programme. It was no wind-up – Cueto was in.

It was to be an eventful week in camp. The team to face Argentina at the Millennium Stadium was named in midweek, Wales No. 8 Michael Owen being given the honour of leading out the Lions for the first time in a Test match on home soil. It was a box-office call, designed to acknowledge the Grand Slam champions and the Welsh public.

The game only came about because the Lions needed to raise cash. As good a job as Feehan had done in the marketplace, the costs were enormous. Hence the game. It was a break with tradition. You might argue that it undermined the noble concept of the Lions coming together and heading into hostile terrain as one band of brothers to defend the honour of the cause. They had no past as a group of blokes, nor a future. They were defined solely by their deeds on foreign fields. It's a fair line of argument. Play one match and get a few million and before you know it, there's a push for two warm-up games and a few more quid in the coffers.

Those who were in Cardiff for the game, however, were much taken by the wonderful bubbly cheer of the crowd – at 61,569 the biggest of the tour, given that stadium capacity in New Zealand is lower than it is in Europe. The face-painted,

merchandise-laden kids came in their thousands to give their heroes a good send-off. Shame about the game. Those hoping for a Barbarians extravaganza were to be profoundly disappointed. It was only in the ninth minute of injury time that Wilkinson slotted the goal that salvaged a modicum of respect, honours finishing even on the scoreboard at 25–25.

Argentina are a splendid rugby nation and the sooner rugby's governing body gets its act together and insists that they are admitted to one of the sport's regular, mainstream competitions, such as the Six Nations or the Tri-Nations, the better. It would be a dereliction of duty if they were not to force the issue. The Pumas had almost pulled out of this prestigious fixture, worried that they might be humiliated. They were without 26 front-line players, many of them still plying their trade with clubs in France. 'We are used to coping with adversity,' said captain Felipe Contepomi, who led his men with typical forthright gusto.

Was there any mitigation for the Lions, who looked edgy, cramped and out of sorts? Not really. Time and again they were turned over. Time and again they were beaten at the breakdown. There were only a handful of genuine Test contenders in their ranks, men such as Wilkinson (one of a very few to shine), lock Danny Grewcock, flanker Lewis Moody, full back Geordan Murphy perhaps, and back-row forward Martin Corry. The Leicester man had hardly dropped a ball all season. He fumbled twice in glaring circumstances. So, too, did Ireland centre Gordon D'Arcy, the man of the moment in 2004 when he had taken the Six Nations by storm. D'Arcy had only played half an hour's international rugby in the 2005 season, groin and hamstring injuries curbing his involvement. He looked jittery, as did many others.

Wilkinson, who scored 20 points, was the only one in decent nick. It was his lovely thrust and offload in the tackle that helped send Ollie Smith to the try line in the 16th minute, a forceful riposte to a livewire opening by the Pumas that had seen them rattle up 13 points without reply in as many minutes. This burst included wing Jose Maria Nunez Piossek touching down and fly half Federico Todeschini adding the conversion. Todeschini's eye was as faultless as his opposite number's, he too ending up with 20 points.

There were to be further concerns for the Lions before they boarded their flight south. Jason Robinson was sent back home the day before departure to tend his wife, Amanda, who was expecting their fourth child. Woodward hoped to have him out in New Zealand by early June. Nothing was certain, though. 'There is a question mark there,' admitted Woodward, who

BELOW The 2005 British and Irish Lions squad and coaching team line up at the Vale of Glamorgan Hotel ahead of their departure for New Zealand.

was also without the two French-based players, Clermont Auvergne's Stephen Jones and Toulouse's Gareth Thomas, who joined up when their French Championship duties were over. 'We have been aware of the situation with Jason for a few weeks. We have pencilled in a return but Jason will not come back until he feels he can come back.'

Woodward has made a virtue of being prepared for the unexpected. A smooth passage rarely happens in sport. If it were that simple then we'd all be coaches. It is those who react best to hassle and inconvenience that tend to thrive.

Woodward did his Henry V bit as the squad packed their bags ready for the ride to London and the flight to New Zealand. It was an impressive rallying cry: 'We'll be very happy if New Zealanders look at that scoreline from the Millennium Stadium and take comfort from it,' said Woodward. 'I have a simple message for those people that await us in New Zealand. I know already from my time spent with this squad that we have the makings of a great Test side. I can tell them also that this is the best prepared squad in the history of the Lions. There will be some of the finest players in the world on that plane tonight. Over the weeks ahead we are going to make them into a world-class team. I believe passionately that we can do that. We all know the enormity of the challenge. No one needs to tell us how tough it is going to be. This trip has been more than a year in the planning. And, now that we are under way for the greatest rugby adventure that any squad or any coach can face, my message to all Lions supporters is very simple: we will do all in our power to meet the challenge.'

Wales pin-up boy Gavin Henson, he of the celebrity girlfriend, had added a henna-style dye to his spiky head of hair. 'It's to match the shirts,' said Henson, part Clint Eastwood in delivery, part Vidal Sassoon. 'You've got to look the part.'

Each to their own. New Zealand awaited.

BELOW The historic Lions against Argentina match in Cardiff ended in a 25–25 draw. Here skipper for the night Michael Owen (right) and scrum half Chris Cusiter stand by as referee Stuart Dickinson readies the packs for a scrum.

Forward pack.

DHL – Official Sponsor of the 2005 New Zealand Lions Series.
Visit us at **www.dhl.com**

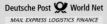

Size is not enough. You've got to be *quick* and *agile* in this game.

While the Lions have been hunting glory, Artemis have been hunting Profits. Just like their leonine counterparts our hunters rely on agility and speed of thought to hit their targets in the investment world. Along with a steady nerve to convert their chances. If you'd like to try your hand at a new sport why not come hunting Profits with us? For contact details see below.

Fig.1
A typical
PROFIT

ARTEMIS
The PROFIT Hunter

Tel: *0800 092 2051*   E-mail: *investorsupport@artemisfunds.com*   Web: *www.artemisonline.co.uk*

2 ▌Up and Running

Money – it buys you a better class of enemy. It didn't take long for a whole battalion of hostile forces to gather on the New Zealand horizon, ready to jib and jibe about the prospects of the 2005 tourists. Laurie Mains let rip in his usual cheerful fashion. John Mitchell had a little dab too. Former coaches both, their take was the same – a 3–0 whitewash for the All Blacks. Well, knock me down with a feather, there's a surprise.

A s Lawrence Dallaglio was to remark a few days later when apprised of Mitchell's comments: 'That wasn't what he said when I bumped into him the other day.'

Private views and public consumption – the worlds don't often collide. The Lions weren't just playing 15 blokes in black. They were up against an entire country. As usual in New Zealand. Professionalism has changed many things. The musketeer mentality – one for all and all for one –

had not changed down where rugby is the nation's sporting fix.

Some of the adverse comments might well have been based on sound foundations. Others were prompted by less savoury inclinations – an envious, chippy, bitter-and-twisted outlook that said more about those delivering their damning verdicts than it did about the object of their ire.

The Lions did have a bloated cast list. 'Mind-boggling' is how former All Black No. 8 Murray

Skipper Martin Corry slides home to score the first Lions try against Taranaki at the Yarrow Stadium.

Mexted described it when doing the voice-over for the Lions first public training session of the tour at North Harbour Stadium in Albany.

The Lions had been in town for four days and had put on their best face. Well, for the most part. They had dutifully attended the arrival press conference, although a three-hour delay didn't endear them to the locals. They then decamped two days later for the formal Maori Welcome in Rotorua, the venue for the opening fixture the following weekend against Bay of Plenty. The whole exercise was designed to show that the Lions were prepared to go out to meet the public.

BELOW 'Form an orderly queue, please.' Gordon Bulloch signs a range of items during the Lions public training session at Albany's North Harbour Stadium. **FACING PAGE** Bill Beaumont, the Lions tour manager, faces the traditional challenge from Maori warrior Richard Wharerahi at the Tamatekapua Welcome House, Rotorua.

It was all carefully choreographed. As was so much of what the Lions did. And therein lay a problem. So big was the entourage – precise numbers were always difficult to pin down given that there invariably seemed to be yet another figure in Lions kit in and around the hotel that you'd never clapped eyes on before – that perhaps it was necessary to have every movement scripted.

It led to an air of falseness at times, notably at the public session at Albany. Woodward had been intent on showing that his men were not going to repeat the mistakes of the 2001 Lions: he was going to get his players into the community to experience local culture.

On Sunday it was the Maori experience. On Tuesday it was the schoolkids' day out, with a few thousand bussed into the morning session. It was a well-intentioned gesture but came over as too slick, too stage-managed, too controlled. The Lions arrived to great fanfare, giant screens showing the official, soft-focus tour video, with each player

introduced to a backdrop of moody music. The players then went through their paces, all in different groups and on different parts of the field.

There was a warm-up routine involving small gaggles throwing tennis balls in a mocked-up game that resembled netball. On another part of the pitch, the kickers went through their drills, many pairs of eyes invariably focused on pin-up boy Jonny Wilkinson. There were sprinting drills, a bit of line-out play, while pitch-side, BSkyB pundit former Bath and England fly half Stuart Barnes conducted interviews with Woodward and his coaches. Barnes's colleague, Miles Harrison, did a commentary throughout, paying due respect to the role of rugby in New Zealand.

Sky do a tremendous job in presenting rugby as well as projecting it to a wider audience. This venture, though, came over as too syrupy, too hand in glove, too directed. There were times when it felt

patronising, as if the Lions had somehow produced something that the New Zealand public had never come across in their lives before. Far better to have had a normal sort of session, with a bit of touch rugby followed by length-of-the-field drills. The players might then have been able to break off from time to time to sign autographs. They did a few signings as they left, but the public were kept at a distance. Twenty junior players were invited to join in the final routines, which was a nice touch.

That said, the charm offensive went down well with the crowds who braved the intermittent squally showers. The official figures put the attendance at 5000 – another seeming distortion, to judge with the naked eye. Those who turned out for the welcome in Rotorua also had to put up with the elements. Lions manager Bill Beaumont had to endure local customs, the down-to-earth man of the north looking a mite uncomfortable as he accepted

ABOVE 'You can never be too careful ...' Workmen 'black out' the windows of a sports clubhouse overlooking a Lions practice pitch to prevent spying on the tourists' training sessions.

the traditional challenge from Maori warrior Richard Wharerahi clad in his unique bare-bottomed indigenous way. Billy B., meanwhile, was suited and booted in his own traditional Sunday best.

So the Lions did reach out to embrace New Zealand and its diverse culture. But only at given moments. The reason for the mixed reaction to them stemmed from their decision to erect an eight-foot high shield around their training base at Onewa Domain in Takapuna. The screens were designed to shut out prying eyes. There was a persistent rumour doing the rounds in 2001 that the Wallabies had cracked the Lions line-out codes. Given that the series came down to a line-out steal in the vital closing stages of the third Test in Sydney, it's easy to see how paranoia might creep in. Whether the line-out code-cracking was an urban myth or not, Woodward was not going to take any chances. So the doors were closed on training.

He had done the same during the Rugby World Cup in Australia, where he had also taken to electronically sweeping the dressing rooms for bugs. Nothing left to chance is the mantra.

Mind you, it didn't always work. New Zealand's *Herald On Sunday* newspaper splashed an exclusive early in the tour, boasting that they had breached security at the Lions harbourside base. One of their reporters had managed to infiltrate the inner sanctum of the team room – funny that there were no pictures accompanying the piece, although there was a revealing reference to the fact that eight laptop computers were spread round the room, displaying varying footage that might have been useful ahead of the tour opener against Bay of Plenty. A sign over one computer read: 'If you want to see how Paul Honiss referees and what he blows penalties for, it's on this laptop.' To judge by the Lions performance that Saturday night in Rotorua, where they failed to get to grips with Honiss' judgments at the breakdown, they must have spent their time on the PlayStation.

The Lions had security minders with them, a couple of them to be seen shepherding Jonny

Wilkinson through the throng at one session. 'It's just common sense,' said Woodward. And so it was, given the huge crowds that tend to flock round Wilkinson. It then seemed perverse of Woodward to make such a song and dance about Prince William coming out to spend time with the party when he was on official duties in New Zealand. The announcement came with appropriate fanfare before the squad left the UK. It was a poor call. Either the Lions wanted their own space or they didn't. Inviting Prince William in such a public fashion was to ask for trouble further down the line as well as raise charges of hypocrisy.

Woodward claimed the visit was 'a major coup for rugby'. 'I think this is great for the Lions, for rugby in New Zealand and for the sport as a whole,' he added. 'It adds to the charisma of the tour and we should be pretty proud that we can handle this. I really don't see any negatives. Would Prince William be going halfway round the world to support a football team? No.'

Woodward had obviously forgotten the disruption caused in Perth 18 months earlier as England tried to prepare for their crucial World Cup pool game against South Africa. Prince Harry was supposedly in town and television helicopters buzzed England's training pitch looking to get shots of him, somehow overlooking the fact that although the young man might be a lively individual he hadn't quite managed to break into England's World Cup squad.

The Lions were welcome guests in New Zealand, indeed cherished. They didn't need to do much to be loved. If anything, they were guilty of trying too hard. They forced the issue, were too overt at pushing their message. Once again, what might have worked at Westminster was not necessarily appropriate in the land of the blunt-talking. They wanted straight deliveries not spin.

The players were of the same mind. They too were getting increasingly twitchy about Campbell's briefings to them prior to press conferences, feeling that they were being spoken to like schoolchildren. These were bright blokes. They didn't need to be mollycoddled, far less have their strings pulled. Campbell was treading a fine line.

The overbearing Lions branding could grate, too, out in the wider community, as manager Bill Beaumont found when outlining plans for eight Lions to visit the flood-stricken region of Matata in the Bay of Plenty. It seemed a noble initiative until one local journalist asked what benefits the Lions might bring to the devastated community. Building houses, perhaps, or piledriving concrete? Ouch! Well-meaning colonials bearing gifts beware.

By far the most significant touch was the sight of the entire team waiting to applaud the Bay of Plenty opposition down the ad hoc tunnel at the end of the tour opener. One problem. Bay of Plenty were strolling round the far side of the ground milking the applause of their fans after a rousing, if losing, display. The Lions waited and waited. A full five minutes elapsed. No problem. Handshakes all round. It was a simple gesture. And a telling one.

Another thought. England had once been mocked for doing a lap of honour at Old Trafford following defeat against the All Blacks. Eight years later Bay of Plenty followed suit and all of New Zealand thought it fine and dandy. Strange.

So much for the backdrop. The Lions would only really define themselves out on the field. That was how we would remember them. Their first chance to lay down a marker was against Bay of Plenty in Rotorua. Woodward wasted no time in naming his side, bringing forward the date of the announcement by three days.

The pack had a very solid feel about it, with Paul O'Connell and Ben Kay getting the opportunity to show what they had to offer the Lions as a second-row combination. A lot was expected of the flame-haired Munster lock. He had impressive credentials – a hard inner core as well as an athletic ability to roam the field. That said, he had come up short in the Six Nations Championship, rather like Ireland themselves. It was a charge that he wasn't going to duck. He knew that he had to raise his standards.

'For a few of the Irish boys this is the second chance to make a piece of history,' said O'Connell. 'We had hoped to do something special for Ireland in the spring but it didn't happen. My own form was not quite where I would have liked it to have been. I was up for every game but sometimes you can work your socks off and it just doesn't run your way. Looking back on it all, it's fair to say that I perhaps need to make things happen more. That will be true with the Lions for sure. You won't get many cracks at showing what you can do. So you've got to get out there and get it done. I'll prepare for the game as if it were a World Cup final or a Grand Slam decider.'

Strong, honest words. O'Connell was to live up to them. Kay, alongside, also had much to ponder prior to the game. England's World Cup-winning lock had seen his form fall away following that tournament. 'There was a dip although not as big as some people made out,' said Kay, who had recovered from a nerve-jangling departure from Heathrow. His state of mind had had nothing to do with any fear of flying and everything to do with the ever-changing scoreline in Istanbul, where his team, Liverpool, were performing their heroics in the Champions League final against AC Milan. He had to board the flight without knowing the result. He even contemplated buying a hand-held television to try and catch those final dramatic moments. As it was, the wonders of mobile phone texting brought him the good news.

Kay was well aware of the keen fight for places that was about to unfold. 'There is a pecking order so if you have a shocker then you go to the back of the queue,' said Kay, who had mixed and matched with Louis Deacon through Leicester's season for the berth alongside Martin Johnson. 'You need to push yourself to the front of the selectors' minds. You've got one definite chance to press your claim. Yes, that's pressure. But that's what it's all about at this level. You've got to be able to cope with it.'

Woodward had pledged to give everyone a guaranteed starting slot in one of the early games. He stressed that he had an open mind on Test selection. 'Like everyone, I have a team in the back of my mind but I'm so aware of Lions history where players come through to nail a Test spot. It happens on every tour so I can't sit here and predict what the team will be. There will be huge battles in every position. Our aim is winning. It's as simple as that. It doesn't matter how we get there as long as we do get there. The history books of sport only

remember those that win.' Winning ugly, winning pretty – there was to be no preordained plan. In fact, as Woodward put it: 'If we arrive at the first Test with the All Blacks knowing how we're going to play we'll come second.'

There was a solid look to the midfield as well, with Gavin Henson paired with Brian O'Driscoll, and the wings alongside both packed a punch. Mark Cueto intended to make the most of his late call-up for the injured Iain Balshaw, while Wales's Tom Shanklin on the other flank simply nodded in ready agreement when Woodward asked him if he would play wing rather than his customary centre. Shanklin had come through strongly in Wales's Grand Slam campaign, his power and intelligence real assets. Josh Lewsey, meanwhile, was considered in many quarters to offer a more potent threat from full back than Jason Robinson, yet had played most of his rugby for England on the wing.

The half-back combination saw Ireland's Ronan O'Gara paired with Wales's shrewd and energetic Dwayne Peel. O'Gara had only just got himself in shape after recovering from a knee injury. It was the astute management of Paula Radcliffe's physio, Ger Hartmann, that really helped O'Gara recover so well. Having worked so hard to get himself back to fitness, the Munster out-half was not now going to doff the cap to fate by blithely assuming that he was making up the numbers behind Jonny Wilkinson and Stephen Jones. 'There is no greater admirer of Jonny than myself,' said O'Gara. 'For sure, he's probably the standard-bearer here. But unless I'm told otherwise then I believe that there's everything to play for.' And so there was.

The manner in which the Lions began the game suggested that they were going to unload in double-quick time every little goodie they had garnered on the training field. They were three tries up within 13 minutes, playing with verve, sharpness and deep inner belief. The Lions looked as if they were going to send Bay of Plenty packing with the same contemptuous ease that they had shown four years earlier in their Australian tour opener, when they ran up a record 116–10 score in Perth.

That match and the gentle romp a few days later against a Queensland President's XV taught

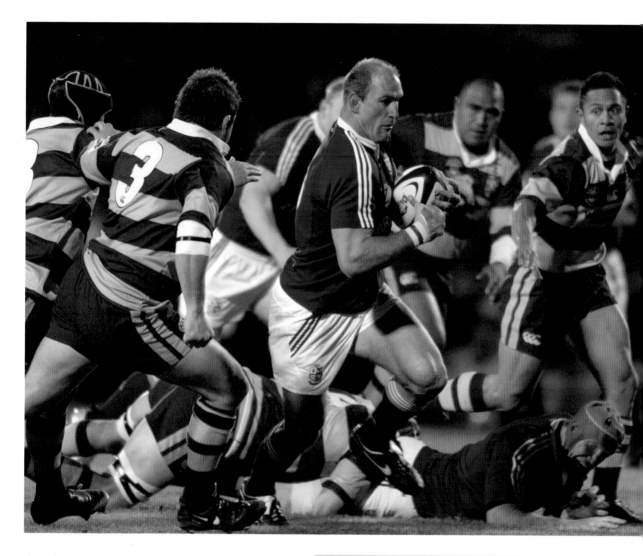

the Lions very little except that Australian rugby outside its major centres was desperately weak. Across the Tasman, things couldn't be more different. Bay of Plenty were on their backsides after that opening salvo, Josh Lewsey ripping them to shreds with his intelligent, sharp-footed attacking play, looking every inch a Test full back as he scored the opening two tries. Sale wing Mark Cueto touched down for the third to give the Lions a 17–0 lead. In a foretaste of what was to come on what proved a disappointing evening for him, O'Gara missed two of the three conversions.

It looked to be all over. And then it all went horribly wrong. In part, the Lions were architects of their own short-lived tumble, even if fate was to give them a cruel nudge over the edge with the crippling injury sustained by Lawrence Dallaglio. By the time Dallaglio was stetchered off the field – 'My kids thought it funny to see Daddy being taken off in a golf cart' was the big fella's typically wry take on the traumatic events – Bay of Plenty had already shown signs that they were not going to buckle under.

The Steamers had a proud record to defend. The previous season had been, according to New Zealand's *Rugby Almanack*, 'the greatest in the history of the Bay of Plenty'. The Bay had been the only team in the NPC never to have held the Ranfurly Shield. That dismal run ended at Eden Park in August when they defeated Auckland 33–28 in the Bay's first successful challenge in 19 attempts. They made one successful defence of the Log O' Wood, against Waikato, before losing to Canterbury in a tight game.

They then went on to make the NPC semi-finals for the first time in its present format. They were not about to roll over for anyone. The Bay were splendidly led by Wayne Ormond, one of those horribly rugged flankers who cause pain and trouble wherever they go. Ormond was to be backed up marvellously by his team – in particular open-side Nili Latu, lock Bernie Upton and debutant fly half Murray Williams.

BELOW Lawrence Dallaglio's tour is over after 23 minutes of the opening fixture against Bay of Plenty, his right ankle broken. **FACING PAGE** Lions scrum half Dwayne Peel races over for a second-half try against Bay of Plenty, urged on by Martyn Williams.

The team also had a raucous following to lift them back into contention. Rotorua's International Stadium was sold out for the first time in 18 years. The 33,000 crowd got their money's worth on what was an uplifting evening. The game was good, with its twists and turns, while the atmosphere at the ground was first rate.

New Zealand have had a tough time convincing the game's administrators that they have the infrastructure to host a Rugby World Cup. The Kiwis lost their sub-host status in 2003 when they refused to fall into line with the RWC commercial programme. RWC called their bluff and stripped them of their rights. By default, we ended up where we should have been all along, with the World Cup held in one country.

New Zealand are bidding for the 2011 World Cup. It's easy to raise reasons why they might come up short on certain criteria. Their Test venues, for example, are way below the capacity levels in the rest of the world. Eden Park is the largest at 45,000. Such restrictions point to a large shortfall in pounds, shillings and pence. Well, revenue should not be the sole driving force underpinning a bid. Let's try culture, appreciation and understanding. They're not bad criteria either. New Zealand can

offer those in spades. Some of that instinctive insight might have been tarnished by the garish, entertainment-driven fluff of Super 12, but for sheer love of the game, the Kiwis are the market leaders. There's another thing – their Test stadiums might fall short but their provincial ones do not. What can England boast outside of Twickenham? Welford Road, Leicester, at 16,000? Kingsholm at 12,000? The opening Saturday saw 33,000 in Rotorua. Four days later in New Plymouth, the Yarrow Stadium hosted 21,000.

The spectators in Rotorua had a whale of a time, which is more than can be said for Dallaglio. The Lions vice-captain was felled by a rotten bit of luck. He was caught awkwardly as he went into a tackle in the 23rd minute, his right leg getting trapped under him. As the play moved away, Dallaglio could be seen on the turf in evident distress. As Brian

O'Driscoll was to say: 'When you hear Lawrence cry out in pain, then you know it's bad.'

It was. A fracture and a dislocation and ligament damage – game, set and match. Dr James Robson, the Lions chief medic and the most respected practitioner in the game, managed to put the ankle back in position on the pitch. 'That eased the pain,' said Dallaglio. We'll take his word for it. It still sounds a horror story. It was for Dallaglio and it was for the Lions. There was to be no denying that unpalatable reality. The Lions could afford to lose virtually any other player in any other position. They could not afford to lose Dallaglio.

He brought an aura and a presence to the Lions forward pack that was beyond the scope of anyone else. The Lions knew that. So, more crucially, did the opposition. Dallaglio was the only player that they would have traded for one of their own. And to think that he was considered a doubt for the tour given that he had retired from international rugby back in September, the then England captain having stood down for personal reasons.

The leadership combination of O'Driscoll and Dallaglio was a potent one. Dallaglio was also a player with a skill set that not many others could match, a strength and awareness of the game that was beyond the scope of his peers. He was in great shape. He had dedicated himself to peaking for the trip. And now it was over, just as it had been four years earlier in Australia when he went home after a couple of games with a cruciate injury.

'You can't compare this to four years ago,' said Dallaglio. 'It's just coincidence that I've had two major injuries in my career and both have happened on Lions tours. It is disappointing because I was feeling in good shape. I felt like I would have been able to make a major impact. I was genuinely excited by the Lions as it has the makings of such a great trip. There is a very strong spirit within the camp and I'm sure that they will be successful.'

He said the right things even when in distress. And did the right things, too. Despite all the trauma of having his tour ended by injury, Dallaglio made sure his number 8 jersey was left on the peg of his Bay of Plenty opposite number, Colin Bourke, who vowed never to wash it.

Dallaglio returned to Auckland by road and underwent surgery immediately to have a plate and five screws inserted in his ankle. He was given a recuperation period of four to six months but dismissed fears his career would be over by vowing to make his return in October.

'I have been very fortunate throughout my rugby career, being fit, the majority of the time, for the big occasions – winning three domestic titles in a row with Wasps, the Heineken Cup and the World Cup with England. Yes, it would have been great to finish this Lions tour but the dice has rolled and I have to accept the situation. I knew my leg had been caught in the ground and it wasn't facing in the right direction. I knew straightaway that my tour was over but I never thought that my career was in doubt. I am under no illusions about the

FACING PAGE Gethin Jenkins (number 1) and Richard Hill hoist lock Paul O'Connell into the evening sky to win clean ball for the Lions against Bay of Plenty.

amount of hard work I am going to face to get fit for next season and I will be very disappointed if I am not back playing by October. I am now looking forward to a break – I just didn't think it would be this kind of break!'

The measure of his loss was apparent for all to see in Rotorua. In his absence the Lions went walkabout, losing their shape and their intensity. They slipped off tackles, no one more glaringly than O'Gara, who ruined his promising start by falling apart defensively in that second quarter. The Irishman regrouped well after the interval, changing his game to drop deeper and drill kicks into the corner. The strategy was to deliver the much-needed victory for the Lions, but we wanted to see more from O'Gara. Instead he crumpled under pressure.

By half-time Bay of Plenty were back in business, tries from Colin Bourke and Murray Williams helping them to level the issue at 17–17. The cheers as they went down the tunnel were heartening for them and troubling for the opposition. The Lions were much tighter in the second half. They kept it simple and they got due reward. Even then, they had to scrap away for it. It was not until the last ten minutes that they made it safe on the scoreboard, Dwayne Peel and Gordon D'Arcy crossing for tries to add to an earlier one from Shanklin.

Peel showed that the promise he had displayed during Wales's Grand Slam campaign was no fluke. Part Rob Howley, part Terry Holmes, Peel has snap, strength and composure in his play. As with Lewsey, Peel looked to have inked in his Test selection.

There were encouraging signs elsewhere, notably in the second row, where O'Connell in particular came through strongly. Kay did his cause no harm either with a couple of fine line-out steals. Martyn Williams was busy and effective on the open side in what was his first competitive outing in six weeks. It was not until the heavyweight brigade of

Andrew Sheridan and Steve Thompson came on, however, that the scrummage was able to assert any sort of authority. The pair of them did their own chances no end of good in their brief appearances.

In the centre Gavin Henson was clever and able in equal measure. He has one hell of a boot on him and he used it to good effect to relieve pressure at various times. It was a surprise when Woodward chose to substitute him for D'Arcy ten minutes from time. The reasoning was that Woodward, prompted by Eddie O'Sullivan, felt that the combination of three Irishmen in midfield – O'Gara, D'Arcy and O'Driscoll – might have a better chance of wrapping up the game. They did so. However, if Henson and O'Driscoll were to ever forge a Test-type relationship, then they would need all the game time on offer. They had shown glimpses of a burgeoning relationship, although there were also flaws in their play, particularly in defence.

O'Driscoll himself missed a couple of tackles, rare blemishes. He was guilty of trying too hard, getting involved just to express his own commitment. He was honest enough afterwards to admit that it had been a mixed bag for him and his team. But they had got off to a winning start, 34–20, and that was the overriding objective. They could move on, which was more than could be said for poor Dallaglio.

Gareth Jenkins had presented the jerseys to the team before the game. It has become the norm these days to come up with some sinew-stiffening ploy prior to important occasions. It's not the worst idea, although you do wonder how deep the well of superstar figures actually is. Some of them will be on their second tour of duty before long.

Jenkins, though, was a great choice. A popular man, a first-rate coach and an eloquent, passionate speaker, he could invest asking for a cup of tea in the morning with emotion. He has soul and he has charisma.

What he didn't have was an international cap never mind a Lions tour on his CV. Perfect. If anyone could get across to the players just what heritage they were representing, it was him, the man who got close but nowhere near close enough. It's the absence of something that makes you appreciate its worth. He knew what it all meant. By the time he had finished in the dressing room the players did too.

Jenkins, 54, a grafting, crafting flanker in his time, had put his whole being into Llanelli. His club record stood comparison with the best, with six Welsh Cup victories to his name, a league and cup double as well as several, stirring, heart-stopping forays into Europe.

He had been passed over for the Wales job, rebuffed without so much as a by your leave. Woodward's call to arms was due recompense, not that sentiment ever entered into the equation. There are times when Woodward comes across as excitable and intemperate. It's no more than a front, albeit a genuine one; but the real man is one driven by attention to detail. He wanted Jenkins because he believed he fitted the brief – technically sound and temperamentally on the right wavelength. Jenkins made a good double act with Ian McGeechan in the midweek team, with former Ireland defence coach Mike Ford, a disciple of Phil Larder, working alongside them. The three men gave off the right vibes.

They had their first stint at the coalface coming up in New Plymouth. The team did its preparation back in Auckland. Woodward had decided that the strain of constant packing and unpacking – always on the move, always adapting to new surroundings – placed too big a strain on players' reserves of energy. So a complicated matrix was drawn up whereby teams went their different ways at different times depending on which phase of game preparation they were in. On match days the whole squad would be in attendance, the non-playing mob often flying in to attend community projects in the morning before flying straight back by charter plane after the game so that they could get either their full rest or stuck into the final part of training for their next match.

It was all laid out on a platter for the players. What they lost was the sense of a travelling circus hitching its wagons and rolling on into the next town. What they gained was maximum opportunity for work and rest. In essence, Woodward was ensuring that they had no excuses for failure.

Selection at this stage of the tour was quite straightforward. It was a question of giving everyone in the squad game time. Those who had not played against either Argentina or Bay of Plenty would get their chance against Taranaki. Most of those decisions were made before the tour got under way, the coaches deciding in advance the combinations they wanted to see tried out. Only injury modified those plans.

This was effectively the last game in which the selectors would honour their pledge to give every player a starting slot. It was now or never for many. Those who hadn't yet had that opportunity were front-row forwards Andrew Sheridan, Steve Thompson and Julian White and half backs Matt Dawson and Stephen Jones.

The players were acutely aware of what was at stake. Vice-captain Will Greenwood may have been round the block a few times in his distinguished career, but he had yet to play in a Test for the Lions despite making ten appearances on two tours of duty. A nasty head injury did for him in South Africa in 1997, while various ailments scuppered him four years later. 'I don't look back with any regrets and if all I end up being on this trip is a bag-carrier then I'll bite your hand off to do that just as long as we can win the series,' said Greenwood. 'Winning the series is all that matters, not me ticking off boxes as to what I have and have not done in my career.'

He knew that he had only managed to scuffle his way into this tour party through the tradesmen's entrance, his patchy season further undermined by a shoulder injury. 'Was I pleasantly surprised? Delighted, more like.' Greenwood took his place next to young Ollie Smith in the centre.

There was an air of the unknown about certain combinations – the tight-head John Hayes packing down next to the fiery if diminutive Andy Titterrell, and the half-back pairing of Scotland's Chris Cusiter with Charlie Hodgson – as there always is on Lions trips. Which way would the dice roll? By the end of another intriguing evening we knew that Hayes was surplus to Test requirements, while Hodgson gave notice of his intention to push Jones and Wilkinson all the way.

There was to be a lot of attention focused on the back row, notably on the figures of Leicester teammates Martin Corry and Lewis Moody. Wales No. 8 Michael Owen, who captained the Lions against the Pumas, was getting as much action as he could before briefly returning home for the birth of his second child.

Corry had the honour of leading the team down the tunnel, a prelude to what the Lions management hoped would be a commanding display on the field, all the more of a necessity now that Lawrence Dallaglio was out of the tour. Corry, so forceful, so influential for club and country, had been off colour in Cardiff against the Pumas. The Lions needed men to step into the breach, and Corry had the potential to do just that.

He galvanised the troops beforehand, gave the final captain's exhortation and burst out of the dressing room to lead the charge onto the field. It was only as he lined up for the anthems that it dawned on him that he had blundered. 'I caught sight of the face of Louise Ramsay, the Lions manager, who is brilliant in organising every last little detail,' said Corry afterwards. 'It was then I realised that in my pumped-up state I'd forgotten to take the Lion mascot with me on the field. It was there beside her. Oh bollocks!'

Corry did little else wrong that evening. It took a long while for the forward pack to find their range, but they were eventually able to get on top of a very spirited opposition. Taranaki, like most of the provincial opposition the Lions faced, were not to make that process easy. They were a less rounded side than Bay of Plenty, less capable of striking from all parts of the field, but they did have solid foundations up front, where two All Blacks led the resistance. Veteran prop Gordon Slater, who played against the Lions 12 years ago, and hooker Andrew Hore, who was unlucky not to make the cut for the present All Black squad, were to test the Lions at the set piece.

Taranaki also had their moments behind the scrum, where the deft, slippery skills of Lifeimi Mafi in the centre made sure that the Lions midfield defence had to be on its toes. The Lions were caught napping, though, just before half-time,

when flanker Chris Masoe was able to sneak behind a pile of bodies to pluck the ball up and score.

The Lions trailed 7–6 at the break, Hodgson landing two penalties, and had been made to work very hard for that minimal return. However, they gained in authority after the interval to score four tries. Hodgson, with a bright, breezy service from Scotland scrum half Cusiter, mixed up play well, showing none of the frayed nerves and hesitant decision-making that affected him at various times for England. He finished with 16 points.

'Charlie was tremendous,' said Corry, who staked a claim to a Test slot in his usual industrious, no-nonsense way. 'He reads the game so well and has such a rugby brain that even when we struggled a bit his own confidence was not affected. Cream always rises to the top and that's what you saw out there with Charlie. The great thing for the team is that we kept our composure when we were under pressure in the first half.'

It was Corry's try just after half-time that seemed to drain the energy from Taranaki. It took several big-screen replays before video referee Paddy O'Brien felt confident enough to rule that Corry's feet had not been dragged into touch as he scored. 'Even if that try had not been awarded I felt scores would have come soon after,' said Corry.

The bustling purpose of Hodgson, the swift-footed, subtle touches of full back Geordan Murphy with his brace of tries, the slickness of scrum half Chris Cusiter all conspired to help the Lions finish the game in some style, Taranaki's injury-time try from Brendon Watt notwithstanding.

There was also a clever, forceful performance to admire from Wales No. 8 Michael Owen, almost unrecognisable from the fretful, insipid figure that led the Lions against the Pumas at the Millennium Stadium. That responsibility obviously weighed too heavily on the shoulders of the softly-spoken Owen. His ball-handling offered the Lions so many options. It was Owen's lovely wide pass that sent Murphy to the line in the 74th minute.

Hodgson, a hangdog figure at times in what had been a turbulent season for him, played with great authority. Every aspect of his game was on the button. He bossed the show, bringing his men into the line and always looking for the defence-splitting, perceptive pass rather than the safe and predictable one. His tackling, which has been questionable, was also on the mark. Jonny Wilkinson and Stephen Jones remained ahead of him in the rankings, but Hodgson did what he could to make the selectors think again. That is all you can ask.

BELOW 'What did I do, ref?' Taranaki lock Scott Breman collars Chris Cusiter in front of referee Kelvin Deaker as the scrum half takes a quick tap penalty. **FACING PAGE** Lions fly half Charlie Hodgson on the move against Taranaki in what was the Sale man's most complete performance of the season.

The same was true of Cusiter, one aberrant pass apart. The young Scot would have been reaching for the erase button for that moment, his wild fling just before the interval missing Hodgson by about three metres. Martin Bayfield would have struggled to take it. From there Taranaki were to work Chris Masoe over the try line. It was a lone blemish, albeit a costly one. 'That was a real howler and I had to give myself a kick up the backside,' said Cusiter.

Murphy was to keep the selectors thinking, too, his two tries matching the haul of Josh Lewsey against Bay of Plenty. He has the occasional wobbly moment, but his imaginative feel for the game can open up endless possibilities, as was shown when he flicked on for Shane Horgan's 69th-minute try. Murphy's second score of the night was payback for the one harshly ruled out in the first half, touch judge Steve Walsh calling a forward pass from Horgan following a pinpoint cross-kick from Hodgson. No such problems second time around.

The Lions had their frailties, notably in the scrum until Gethin Jenkins replaced John Hayes on the tight-head shortly after half-time. Hayes cut a disconsolate figure. He knew his Test prospects were shot to bits. Andy Titterrell would also have been disappointed that a couple of his throws were adjudged crooked in the first half, although it took the ever-intrusive presence of touch judge Walsh to spot them. The Lions had to weather a typically forthright offering from Taranaki, forcefully led by lock Paul Tito. Mafi was a handful throughout the first half, while Slater and Hore ensured that the Lions knew that they had been in a contest.

Two wins from two starts in New Zealand. The Lions had their failings, but they had addressed them on the field. Insights gained that way are worth their weight in gold.

The Lions headed back to Auckland to prepare for an altogether more strenuous task. The New Zealand Maori loomed on the immediate horizon. Bay of Plenty and Taranaki had given what they had to offer – and stern, resilient stuff it was – but they had tired. The Maori would not tire. That much was certain.

The pace of life in New Zealand may be gentle and meandering. Not on its rugby fields, it isn't. The tour was about to hit overdrive.

BELOW Lions full back Geordan Murphy scores his first try of the evening despite the arrival of Taranaki's Brendon Watt.

AND MAKE ROOM FOR SPORTS

SO YOU CAN SPREAD OUT

*BUSINESS*ELITE HAS NO MIDDLE SEAT

delta.com/uk

*For further information on our BusinessElite® service
from London and Manchester to the U.S., please call 0800 414 767 or visit our website.*

3 ■ Striving to Impress

It's easy to get mixed signals on a Lions tour. New people, new combinations, new concept of touring – it's not difficult to read the runes and come up with a warped perspective. That was the way it was in New Plymouth on the Thursday morning after the Taranaki game. The skies were clear, the airport was open, the copy had been tidied up and filed from the night before and a prompt return to Auckland was anticipated.

It didn't materialise. There was fog at Auckland Airport even though one of the New Zealand producers at Sky Sport swore blind that from his office window in the city all he could see were clear skies. It wasn't his view that mattered. A long stream of miserable hacks bundled their way into hire cars, clapped-out buses and even a camper van to wend their way back to Auckland, a picturesque up-hill-down-dale five-hour journey through one of New Zealand's national parks. All very pleasant unless you happened to be stuck behind that blooming camper van. Given that 1600 camper vans had been booked out across the country to cater for the invading army of Lions fans, there were going to be a lot of disgruntled, slow-moving convoys over the coming days. Or not, perhaps. How often do you get the chance to sniff the roses and admire the scenery? Not often these days.

It was strange being back on a proper touring schedule. Midweek matches. Ah, the glory days of

A defender's-eye view of No. 8 Ryan Jones as he crashes through the Otago defence to score on his Lions debut.

weeks spent on the west coast of Ireland ostensibly covering the All Blacks in Connacht and in reality sampling all the riches that part of Ireland has to offer. Millions of brain cells lay in ruins round that part of the world. The self-inflicted cranial destruction was well worth it.

Such is the wonder of Lions tours. They take you back to how it used to be. And how it should be. There is nothing more boring and frustrating for journo, player and fan alike than the week-long build-up to a Test match, when every coach dances round the truth, when every opposition is to be respected, when no opponent is to be bad-mouthed. How you yearn for someone, just once, to tell it as it really is – that they want to beat the livin' bejesus out of those bastards. But, no, the platitude rules the airwaves.

It was illuminating to listen to Clive Woodward a couple of days before the Otago match. It had been a strained few days on the press front. The media operation had gone into meltdown. A system had been put in place that was simply not working. The master plan, overseen by Alastair Campbell, might have looked OK on paper. In reality, access to players was rushed and frantic, and every conversation with a player was monitored by one of the Lions media corps. It was a recipe for serious friction, with established media men being told to hurry up by someone barely out of short trousers. Never mind punch-ups on the field. There was serious danger of there being punch-ups in press conferences.

It was not that long ago that you could freely mingle with players in hotel lobbies and even in bars and nightclubs. Rumour has it that drink was occasionally taken. What happened on tour, stayed on tour. There was no snitching. That backdrop has changed. The press rarely stay in the same hotels as the players, the players rarely break curfew. Everything is now formalised. People are employed to manage what used to happen naturally – that is, the exchange of comment between grown-ups. Is it a better system? No, it isn't. Trust is a far more potent, productive force than any hand-me-down, top-table sound bite. One is natural, the other contrived. What a waste of money.

The old way was more fulfilling on both sides. If a player resented criticism or misrepresentation, then he told the reporter to his face. It was called communication. Now, we had a crowded huddle here, a snatched ten minutes there, microphones and tape machines thrust forward, questions fired in some poor player's face, the guy staring back like a cornered fox, fending off the rat-a-tat inquisition. And to think the Lions paid good money to come up with that system. No one got anything out of it. Press were shepherded in and shepherded out, with scarcely a pleasantry exchanged with people that you'd known for several years.

You can see why the management might want to keep the press at arm's length. You could argue that it prevented players from being hassled and also ensured that any little titbits stayed in-house. So much for the theory. There is another reality, and that is the one where more profound relationships were formed and confidences were never betrayed. The modern world can be a cold place.

We had agreed to give the Lions their space, even downgrading hotels in Christchurch and Wellington to enable them to be on their own. The consequence was that barriers were erected. Literally so in Wellington, where the situation came to a head. The team and press were, for once, in the same hotel. We arrived to find that the frontage of the building had been screened off, with temporary, concrete-weighted barricades all along the street. There were two tiers of security at the entrance. Meanwhile, guests checking into the five-star establishment arrived in their rooms to find letters from the hotel management pointing out something really important. The communications were to the effect that guests might recognise some well-known people during their stay but please would they refrain from requesting autographs or photographs so that the hotel's atmosphere could be maintained for all those in residence.

It was a PR disaster. The Lions may not have instigated the security but they were to be associated with it. Stories were filed accordingly. There was more. A minor collision in training between a couple of players had been picked up by a news agency back in the UK, misinterpreted and sent out to news desks. The rumour mill took over and while New Zealand slept, some newspapers took it upon themselves to rewrite their man's copy, splashing headlines of brawls in the Lions camp, with talk too of civil war breaking out. Now that would have been news, especially to the Roundheads and Cavaliers who had copyright on such matters.

It was a taxing few days. And all at a time when Woodward showed that he is at his best when asked to make quick decisions. Even though he was taken aback to hear of the discontent among the media, he immediately took steps to address the situation. Players were put up for interview in far more informal, relaxed circumstances. We were all the better for it. Woodward rightly blasted the trumped-up headlines and we all moved on.

He was to take some stick locally as well when the Lions reined back on their meet-and-greet activities in the community down in Otago. It was towards the end of the week when Woodward began to depart from the script. He had been desperately keen to say the right things, too keen in fact. It came over as a convention for the politically correct. He said the right thing too often, about how wonderful it was to be in New Zealand and all that guff.

The Lions had won a few hearts and minds. Good on them, too, for getting out and about. The players enjoyed the forays off-piste. But there is a time and a place. The Test series was looming. It

BELOW John Hayes (left) and Gordon Bulloch (right) practise maintaining low body positions under nets, ahead of the match against Wellington. A minor collision during this training session was erroneously reported in some sections of the media as a bust-up between the two players.

was time to get on the front foot. 'We are on a rugby tour not a community tour,' was Woodward's pointed response at the end of the week to yet another enquiry as to why the Lions were changing their off-field schedules. Quite right.

There was an encouraging moment, too, when Andy Robinson inadvertently spoke of his satisfaction when seeing Wellington flanker Ben Herring forced off at half-time 'having been completely battered' in the words of Robinson. Heartfelt word, that, 'battered'.

Woodward had been in spiky, feisty but good-humoured mood, too, having a dart at those who would write off the Lions. Excellent. Tell it as it is, Clive, not as a Campbell script might have wanted it. All that was for later in the week.

It all happens quickly on a trip like this. Game, post-mortem, new selection, preview, game. There is no hiding place on these tours, no time to rest, draw breath and regroup. Brilliant. Proper sport. Fair play to Woodward. He had fought for a full itinerary of games to be put in place. The recommendation from the 2001 trip was that there should be fewer games and shorter tours. Woodward argued for the opposite. He wanted to re-establish old principles. He wanted to re-create a sense of the great adventure. He wanted it to be different and special for all concerned. Woodward has never been content with the mundane and run-of-the-mill. He is rarely to be found on the straight and narrow, chugging along safely in the middle lane. Woodward wants everything to be the best that it can possibly be. If that means that at times he overreaches himself, or comes across as fanciful and hot-headed, then so be it. Better to have tried and failed than not to have tried at all.

He wanted the players to get everything they could out of the tour. But he also wanted to win the Test series. So there was to be no reverting to the old routines of hitching wagons and traipsing from town to town, packing bags, laying down sleeping rolls, smashing up a few bars, throwing a few pianos out of windows, and breaking a few hearts before moving on. That was a call too far.

The players came in and out of the venue town as and when their training schedule fitted. It was a complex matrix and there was a danger of the Lions being accused of tokenism as they came and quickly went, but all the bases were touched. The Lions appeared on front pages on arrival in every town. They chose their moments for public appearance, but there was invariably a sense of openness and friendliness from the players.

They too had a slight delay as they made their way back by charter flight to Auckland. At least they didn't get shunted out onto the road. They were back in town by early afternoon, ready to hear the team announcement for the next game against the Maori. There was a buoyant mood in camp, perhaps a misleading one. Two games had been won, two New Zealand provinces laid to rest. It was tempting to float along on a cloud of mild euphoria in that the tour had got off to a decent start, the rotten injury to Dallaglio notwithstanding.

That mood was about to undergo a spot of serious revision. Bay of Plenty and Taranaki had both got stuck in, both caused the Lions early difficulties, but both teams were not the best there was on offer. Each of those teams had at least half a dozen part-timers in their ranks. They could not have hoped to match the Lions for 80 minutes. It was inevitable that the Lions would come through to win. They would have had to be a truly dreadful outfit for that not to have happened.

The New Zealand Maori were something else entirely. They did have a pedigree. And, more importantly, they had all their players available. New Zealand coach Graham Henry agreed to release All Black prospects such as back-row forwards Jono Gibbes and Marty Holah and speedsters Rico Gear and Leon MacDonald.

The All Blacks were also playing that weekend, against Fiji in North Harbour on Friday evening. Henry, though, was happy that the Maori should have a proper crack at the tourists. More's the pity that he didn't adopt the same policy throughout the tour. A few days later in Wellington, there was a tasty fixture on the schedule with the Lions due to play the NPC finalists. Wellington had five hard-hitting, front-line All Blacks in their ranks – captain Tana Umaga, his co-centre, the highly rated Conrad Smith, Ma'a Nonu, and bruising back-row

forwards Jerry Collins and Rodney So'oialo. Of the quintet, only Nonu was allowed to play.

How sad. How cheap. The New Zealanders were devaluing their own show. The Lions had come, rolled up their sleeves and got on with it. They had lost Dallaglio to a cruel twist of fate. That's sport. They were prepared to roll with those punches. The New Zealanders were not. Their main men were wrapped in cotton wool. The Friday evening romp against Fiji in Albany was a mismatch that did no one any good. The score was 91–0, with the new kid on New Zealand's block, wing Sitiveni Sivivatu, scoring a record four tries on debut. So what. The Fijians, God bless 'em, were a shambles. They had run the Maori close in Suva the week before, losing valiantly 29–27, but here, on the road, they simply turned out to make up the numbers.

The fact that it was one of their own, Sivivatu, who did a lot of the damage only served to underline the desperate state of affairs in the Pacific Islands. They breed 'em, they nurture 'em and then they watch as they are cherry-picked by the rapacious agents acting on behalf of New Zealand or Australia. The latter-day Gastarbeiter, the migrant worker looking to earn his corn so as to help those back home, cannot be blamed. He has stomachs to feed.

It was a dispiriting turn of events. 'That just shows the gulf between the rich and the poor,' said Fiji's coach, New Zealander Wayne Pivac. 'It's a cruel way to learn what tier one rugby is all about. We need to do a lot more ourselves before we put all the blame on others.'

The real onus is on the International Rugby Board to get its act together and do something. There have been a lot of well-intentioned words

ABOVE Scotland No. 8 Simon Taylor talks to the press before a training session for the game against New Zealand Maori, in which he was due to play. By the time the session was over, so was the unfortunate Taylor's tour – his hamstring injury had failed to mend.

coming out of Dublin. It's time for decisive action. Elsewhere that weekend, Australia were beating Samoa 74–7, Wales were putting 60 points on Canada, while poor Uruguay were smashed 134–3 by South Africa. A tale of woe and a damning ledger of account for the IRB.

The Lions, meanwhile, were looking to flex some muscle themselves. They were looking to crank through the gears in what had been billed as the unofficial fourth Test. The Maori certainly knew

what was headed their way when the Lions named the heaviest front row ever to pull on Lions shirts (XXXXL), putting together the all-England unit of Andrew Sheridan, hooker Steve Thompson and tight-head Julian White. The custom-built scales to withstand that lot would register some 348kg (54st 10lbs). Woodward wanted to see if the supposed improvements in New Zealand forward play were all that they were cracked up to be.

The front row had some ballast behind, too, with Paul O'Connell and Simon Shaw, drafted onto the tour for the injured Malcolm O'Kelly, locking out together. There was supposed to be a first start also for Scotland No. 8 Simon Taylor, who was finally to get a run after seemingly shaking off a

BELOW The heaviest Lions front row ever – Julian White (left), Steve Thompson and Andrew Sheridan, all of England – stand by to pack down against the New Zealand Maori in Hamilton.

hamstring problem. It was not to be. As flies to wanton boys, the sporting gods play with certain randomly chosen victims. Taylor was one of those. The die was cast for the 25-year-old after the final run-out on the Friday. His whole being must have slumped when he felt a tell-tale twinge. There was to be no match and no Lions tour. For the second trip in succession, Taylor, whose damaged knee ligaments forced him off the tour to Australia after just one appearance (and that as a substitute), was on his way home. Wales's Ryan Jones replaced him.

As for Sheridan, the selection was a massive opportunity. The 26-year-old converted lock-cum-back-row forward had only one cap to his name, as a replacement against Canada in November. He had the size, he had a reputation as a strongman but could he deliver at the highest level? His brief sortie onto the field against Bay of Plenty suggested he could. During Sheridan's 15-minute appearance towards the end of the game, the Lions scrummage was transformed from passive scufflers into mean-minded aggressors. Sheridan now had to show that he could do that from the first whistle.

Sheridan, an unlikely front-row warrior in that he looked so fresh-faced, brooks no equal when it comes to pumping iron. He bench-presses 275kg. 'He'll show anyone up in the gym,' said his club captain, Jason Robinson, after his own delayed arrival in New Zealand. 'He's a beast. Sherri has come on so well this season and really has the bit between his teeth. This environment will bring out the best in him. He'll be itching to get out there against the Maori and show what he can do.'

Sheridan himself is not one to invest his trade with too much mystique. For him, the appeal is all about the one-to-one battle it allows him to pursue. 'Any prop worth his salt takes pride in his scrummaging,' said Sheridan. 'Everything else is of secondary importance.' Spoken as one who fancied the tussle that awaited him. He was up against All Black prop Carl Hayman – no midget himself.

There were a few raised eyebrows locally when Jonny Wilkinson's name was again missing from the starting line-up. The England fly half had yet to appear on New Zealand soil, although he had played a full part in the pre-tour game against Argentina at the Millennium Stadium. There was no great mystery with Wilkinson. He had been on the bench on Wednesday evening against Taranaki, admiring from close quarters the fine work of Charlie Hodgson. Here, it was the turn of the architect of Wales's Grand Slam success, Stephen Jones, to show just why he ought to be to the fore in Woodward's thoughts.

Jones, a late arrival after fulfilling commitments with his French club, Clermont Auvergne, was paired with experienced Lions campaigner Matt Dawson. Outside them the Lions opted for familiarity in the shape of Brian O'Driscoll and Gordon D'Arcy as they looked to settle their preferred midfield.

There was a diverting bit of pre-match action to contend with before the Lions headed down to Hamilton. Woodward spent Friday afternoon in talks with referee Steve Walsh, who had been embroiled in a World Cup dust-up with England and who was to be in charge against the Maori. Woodward was at pains to clarify just how much advice and instruction a referee should receive from his touch judges.

Both Lions games so far had seen constant interference from touch judges, who were linked electronically to the referee. 'We're not making an issue of this,' said Woodward, whose sole objective in raising the matter was to do just that. 'We just want to see the referee referee the game. I'm surprised at the amount of input there is. Something has got to be sorted out. I'd prefer the touch judge to be watching what happens behind the ball. If he's watching the ball then he might miss something off the ball. If there were an incident then you want to make sure that they get the right person.'

That is exactly what didn't happen during the game against Taranaki. Following a scuffle between Taranaki captain Paul Tito and Lions lock Danny Grewcock, touch judge Paul Honiss misidentified the Lions player as Donncha O'Callaghan. Honiss advised that a yellow card was an option. It was only when the players were called together that the referee, Kelvin Deaker, realised just who had been involved and simply gave them a ticking-off. A minor incident like that could become a major turning point.

A three-man panel of Deaker, Honiss and Walsh, all international referees, were rotating duties during this part of the tour. Walsh ran foul of Woodward during the 2003 World Cup when he was involved in a touch-line spat with fitness coach Dave Reddin. Walsh made judgment calls on several matters when touch-judging against Taranaki. 'We have no issues with the officials,' said Woodward. 'But it must be very difficult for the referee to do his job when there is so much going on in his ear. It's just common sense. If you want three referees out there then you might as well divide the pitch into three with one for each segment. Touch-judging is an art and referees don't necessarily make the best touch judges.'

The Maori were keeping their counsel. Unlike most teams they don't bother trading in the usual verbals. Their team culture is entirely different, Barbarians-like in some ways although founded on something far more spiritual, far more profound. The point of difference, the umbilical cord, is the *whakapapa*, or genealogy, that links members of the team. Team protocol insists on a connection to *tikanga Maori*, a belief in Maori culture and customs. They have their own ways, their own bonding and their own haka – 'Timatanga' tells the story of young warriors and chiefs declaring their ambition for knowledge, unity and excellence.

This was to be a landmark game in their history on what was a special occasion for two members of the group in particular – fly half Carlos Spencer and coach Matt Te Pou. He was stepping down after ten years in charge, a proud man and a force for good in rugby. Spencer, too, is a Maori by birth and by nature. He had been on his travels round the world, turning out for the Barbarians in the UK and flying straight back from Martin Johnson's testimonial match at Twickenham to join the group. This was to be his last game before he packed his

bags and headed to Northampton. Spencer was only on the bench but was certain to get game time.

The Maori had never beaten the Lions in seven attempts, stretching back to 1930. It was evident from the early stages of the game that the record was about to be put to rights. In front of another packed house, at the Waikato Stadium in Hamilton, the Maori played with real snap and devil right from the first whistle. No surprise there. But then they kept playing. And playing. Where other teams had faded and so failed, the Maori grew bigger and more confident. It was to be a sobering night for the Lions as the Maori won 19–13.

There was less than a converted try between the sides on the scoreboard; in truth, there was a chasm

RIGHT Leon MacDonald is on his way to score the New Zealand Maori try despite being closed down by Gordon D'Arcy (12) and Brian O'Driscoll.

in bite, drive and precision. It was a six-point hammering, a reality that the Lions made no attempt to mask even though they almost stole it at the death, and might have done so were it not for an off-the-ball block on Josh Lewsey.

Woodward admitted that it would have been a travesty if the Lions had nicked it. He conceded that they had been well beaten, especially at the breakdown. He pledged to change the priorities in training. No more soft-pedalling. 'We are getting out-hit so something has got to happen,' he said. 'The breakdown area is the biggest concern. There seemed to be a lot more black shirts there than red. Maybe it's time to up the ante in training. We need to stop making excuses and front up.'

The Lions had neither the personnel nor the strategy to cope with an admirably fervent performance from the Maori, roared to the rafters by a 30,000 capacity crowd as they nailed their first ever win over the Lions. The tourists certainly had no one who could match the stature or influence of Maori back-row forwards captain Jono Gibbes (a concoction of famous former Lions names that gives you an apposite indicator of just what he had to offer) and open-side Marty Holah.

Lions flanker Martyn Williams gave his customary sweat and bruised flesh to the cause, but he was twice penalised for infringing in desperation and twice driven backwards by Holah. The fault did not lie entirely at Williams' door, although the

Lions did not have an identikit No. 7 in the locker. Lewis Moody has the energy and enthusiasm but not the control or subtlety, while Back has the craft and guile but not necessarily the legs and lungs. And Richard Hill? Still finding his range after the long lay-off.

The breakdown phase of play was an embarrassment for the Lions. 'It was problematical for us,' said coach Eddie O'Sullivan. 'We were sloppy.' It would have helped, of course, for the pack to get there quicker. And for that to happen, the tight play had to be become more emphatic and decisive. Patience was running out with Steve Thompson's waywardness at crucial line outs. Two throws missed the mark.

The Lions simply did not drive the opposition back on their heels. 'They seemed to have more aggression than us all over the field' was the blunt assessment of Ireland lock Paul O'Connell. Small wonder, then, that the back line faltered and crabbed. Brian O'Driscoll, his swift-footed late try excepted, looked burdened and fretful, two sliced punts suggesting he was less than settled within himself. The relationship with Gordon D'Arcy did not gel, and these are men who know each other well. The Lions were chasing shadows throughout the game. Only clever, clawing defence kept the Maori down to one try, although Leon MacDonald did break through four attempted tackles en route to that 58th-minute score.

Loose-head prop Andrew Sheridan was yellow-carded for taking a swipe at Maori centre Luke McAlister just before the interval. No dispute with that judgment. However, Sheridan did not return,

BELOW Skipper Brian O'Driscoll crosses for a late try against New Zealand Maori, but the home side held out for a famous victory. **FACING PAGE** Lions full back Josh Lewsey and Maori wing Caleb Ralph challenge for a high ball.

ABOVE Jonny Wilkinson, on his first Lions outing in New Zealand, confers with his half-back partner, Dwayne Peel, during the 23–6 victory over Wellington at the Westpac Stadium.

Woodward deciding to send on Gethin Jenkins once the bin time was served. Sheridan, though, was just beginning to get a nudge on his opposite number, All Black Carl Hayman, another bear of a man. Why not let the rookie Sale prop get more game time? Woodward said that it was always in his mind to let Jenkins loose. An ankle injury to Sheridan declared later in the week hinted at a different version of events.

The Lions headed back to Auckland to pack their bags for the South Island. They were to be based for a fortnight in Christchurch, even though the next game was at the tip of the North Island in the capital, Wellington. There was plenty to ponder on the flight south.

A rallying blast of bugles sounded from the Lions camp on Sunday evening as Woodward summoned several front-line players to the cause for the midweek game. Once again, the head coach was Boxing and Coxing with convention. Tradition dictates that you run your first team seven days out from the Test. Here Woodward seemed to be getting his preference in early.

There was a first Lions outing in New Zealand for fly half Jonny Wilkinson, so too for Neil Back, itching to make amends for his recent indiscretion, which had resulted in a four-week ban for punching. Also on the roster were two other men who had captained their countries, wings Jason Robinson of England and Wales's Gareth Thomas, both of them, too, pulling on the Lions jersey for the first time on this trip.

Lions captain Brian O'Driscoll was launched back into the fray in an attempt to boost morale in the wake of the troubling defeat. The Ireland centre, struggling to find form himself, was paired with Gavin Henson in a back line that had the air of a shadow Test combination. Josh Lewsey stepped out for his second game in four days, while Dwayne Peel partnered Wilkinson at half back. Tasty. This lot had an air of conviction about them, although there was still form to find and relationships to nurture. 'I need to play well to get the best out of those around me, helping the team to perform so that we can have smiles on our faces come Thursday morning,' said Wilkinson. 'I've got to give it everything I've got.'

Wilkinson always has to contend with more than just the grizzled lot in opposition trying to knock him off his stride. He woke on Monday morning to find Gloucester and France defence coach Dave Ellis – now billing himself as being firmly in the All Black camp, which was news to New Zealand RFU officials – suggesting in the New Zealand media that he was no longer up to the mark. 'Wilkinson is a great kicker and great attacker but there are big question marks over his defence,' said Ellis. 'He used to rush up and take players head-on, ball and all. But he's had to change his style and he's now missing a lot of tackles.'

Wilkinson was to laugh at the suggestion. 'I haven't changed anything,' he said. 'What has changed is the circumstances in the teams I'm playing in. It's just a question of working yourself into position.'

There was a lot of brow-furrowed debate about the Lions frailties at the breakdown. They were being beaten for pace, punch and numbers. Small wonder that they were struggling for worthwhile possession. Neil Back to the rescue. Well, that was one simplistic way of looking at it. The problem was actually far more complex. Back, though, was just the man to bolster self-belief as well as inject craft into the Lions approach in and around the contact. He was an unlikely knight in shining armour given that at the age of 36 he was on the verge of becoming the oldest man ever to play for the Lions in a Test match. To achieve that landmark he needed to play in the third and final Test, when he would be 36 years and 174 days of age. Wales prop Charlie Faulkner was 36 years and 170 days when he played for the Lions against Fiji in Suva in 1977.

The Lions had struggled for fluency and impact. Back had the knowledge, as well as the powers of organisation, to do something about that. Woodward was not slow to point that out. 'The last time Backie played Richie McCaw he came out on top,' said Woodward, referring to England's galvanising win over New Zealand in Wellington prior to the 2003 World Cup. 'I'm looking forward to seeing a supercharged performance from a guy wearing a red number 7 shirt.'

So too was Back himself, the pent-up energy of kicking his heels for the past month following his ban for punching Joe Worsley ready to explode into productive action. 'I'm desperate to play,' said Back, who retired from England duties in 2004 after being left out by Woodward and would hang up his playing boots altogether following this final fling. 'I back myself totally both physically and mentally. Even though I regret getting involved in something that prevented me from playing the thing that I love to do, I look at every setback positively and I've been able to get away from all the knocks and bangs. I'm in prime shape and ready for Wednesday's match. To get in the Test side would be a real challenge but it's one that I've met before and done. It holds no fear for me at all.'

Back refused to reduce the debate about the Lions failings to a single focus on the role of the open-side. 'It's not just about who happens to be wearing the number 7 shirt,' said Back. 'It's a contentious area. What we've got to do is concentrate on clearing out past the ball, being more physical there. It's all about commitment and an appreciation of what needs to be done. I don't see rectifying it as a problem at all.'

The contact area did improve against Wellington. But not a lot else did as the Lions spluttered to a 23–6 victory. There were different takes on the merits of the performance. The charitable view was that the Lions were masters of disguise, concealing their hand until they reached the first Test in Christchurch. The less flattering slant on another slipshod, faltering victory was that they were still having trouble locating each other on the radar and were fast running out of time to rectify the failings.

Wellington coach John Plumtree reckoned that the All Blacks would have put 60 points on his side.

ABOVE The excellent Gethin Jenkins delivers a shuddering tackle on Wellington's Shannon Paku. **FACING PAGE** Gareth Thomas chips ahead and sets off in pursuit to score the second Lions try against Wellington late in the second half.

In essence, they would have made much better use of ball and opportunity. The Lions sniffed the line on several occasions but were not able to land the kill. The search for the potent thrust, for swagger and strut, continued. The clock was ticking.

But they did win. That was a notable consolation after a patchy performance on what was a typically filthy night in New Zealand's capital city. With the rain sluicing down and the wind chilling the bone, handling was always going to be tricky. Even so, the Lions ought to have coped better than they did.

Too much of their passing was sloppy, either landing behind the man or at an awkward angle. Their openings would be far more limited in the Tests. Their delivery had to be a lot better.

The Lions had enough possession and position to have won comfortably against a Wellington side deprived of the services of four All Blacks and below strength in three more positions. There was a measure of justice applied to the scoreboard by a late chip-and-chase try from Gareth Thomas, but the stark reality was that the Lions did not shred the opposition as they should have done. They had the ball; they did not have the edge. The build-up had some shape and some intent. It was the execution that let them down. Martin Corry was within inches of the line in the first half, while Ben Kay following up was too rushed to close the deal.

What the Lions did have was an unforgiving, hard-working scrum. The line out, too, was more productive. Wales loose-head Gethin Jenkins had an outstanding game in all phases and played himself into the Test team. He not only did his chores in the tight, he threw himself into the fray round the field. He was on hand to take an inside pass from Martin Corry to canter to the try line in the 36th minute, the opening carved initially by the impressive Dwayne Peel. Julian White, Jenkins' mate on the other side of the scrum, was a real cornerstone. Quite how referee Paul Honiss found fit to penalise the dominant Lions scrum was beyond the ken of many observers. Baffling, and worrying given that the Lions want to scrum. Shades of the Wallabies in the World Cup.

There was an intriguing call to make at hooker, where Ireland's Shane Byrne bedded down in the front row and threw well in the line out, a rash 60 seconds apart when a couple of line outs misfired. Steve Thompson had the power game, but Byrne was the steadier option.

Locks Danny Grewcock and Ben Kay were industrious, while the back-row unit was influential in all sorts of areas, notably the breakdown. The Lions had been put on their backsides by the New Zealand Maori. Here they competed with more vigour and intelligence, forcing a couple of turnovers and proving far more effective.

Woodward brought on Stephen Jones for the last quarter in place of Gavin Henson, with Wilkinson moving infield to inside centre. The experiment was not conclusive, like so much during the course of the evening. Woodward could go either way as regards Test selection. Henson is solid as well as troublesome. He also has the kick of a

mule. Jones, though, is a shrewd operator at fly half. Wilkinson, playing his first game in three weeks, had a mixed evening. He was out of kilter with his field-kicking, missing a couple of penalties, too, as well as a dropped goal in the opening seconds. His passing game was not as assured as normal either, in keeping with the off-key tone of play in general. He looked short of match practice.

Two of the back three, Jason Robinson and Gareth Thomas, were making their first starts of the tour. Robinson had little to do and did not manage to work himself into the game. Thomas hurled himself around, finding space, cutting angles; he deserved his 77th-minute try. The Toulouse wing would have been far less pleased with the way he let Ma'a Nonu slip down the narrowest of blind-side gaps early in the second half, Josh Lewsey eventually rescuing the day.

The quest for a definitive performance continued. The portents were not too auspicious, but nor should the verdicts be too damning or premature. The Lions evolve. They don't just miraculously appear as a rounded side.

The Lions ought to have won more comfortably but were unable to sustain any continuity on a rain-lashed evening. 'It wasn't flawless but we were probably just one pass away from scoring three or four tries,' said captain Brian O'Driscoll. 'The ball was like a bar of soap.' Wellington coach Plumtree, who coached Gavin Henson when at Swansea, was not overly impressed by the Lions performance. 'They are going to have to play a lot more rugby to beat the All Blacks,' he said.

Even though the hour was late, there was still more action to come as manager Bill Beaumont warned afterwards that the Lions ethos was being devalued by the All Blacks refusing to release players. 'As the situation stands there is a threat to the Lions as a touring side,' said Beaumont, who is also chairman of the Lions committee. 'For that concept to survive the Lions have to be playing against the best players.'

Beaumont used the formal post-match banquet to air his views and found support from many New Zealanders who also want to see their best players put on show round the country. 'If we don't get this sorted then I can see a situation where a Lions coach will come down here and just focus on playing three Test matches,' said Beaumont. 'Either that, or he'll have a 22-man squad for the provincial games and a different one wrapped up in cotton wool for the Test series. That would be against the whole ethos and history of the Lions but that is what could happen.'

Implicit in the statements was a sense that the All Blacks were hiding themselves away from the

tourists. The Lions management appeared to relish the opportunity to put that shot across the bows, although it has to be said that the players would rather have played. Wellington flanker Jerry Collins asked to but was denied the chance.

Beaumont was also hugely concerned that the English clubs might refuse to release players so readily for a tour next time, or to re-jig the playing calendar in a Lions year, if the provincial games were to be downgraded by absentees. 'I can imagine people questioning the worth of taking players away for six weeks if they are not playing against the best,' said the man who led the North to victory over New Zealand at Otley in 1979, a week before taking on the All Blacks at Twickenham.

BELOW Ryan Jones and Simon Easterby on the rampage during the Lions 30–19 victory over Otago at Carisbrook, a win that was due in great measure to the dominance of the tourists' back row.

Worthy as Beaumont's argument was, there were kinks in it. There had been nine All Blacks, current and past, on view for the New Zealand Maori the previous weekend. That game, though, was an exception. The Lions also simply cannot do without games. They cannot just jet in for a Test series. As we were seeing on this trip, they need game time to find their own identity. No matter what the calibre of the opposition, the Lions have to play matches.

Next up were Otago, a side with a proud record against the Lions – five victories in twelve attempts. They too were without three All Blacks – tight-head Carl Hayman, lock James Ryan and hooker Anton Oliver, although the last-mentioned would not have played whatever the circumstances, given that he had to withdraw from contention for the Test side when his calf injury failed to heal.

Woodward opted for an overtly second-string side. A clutch of those selected, nevertheless – full back Geordan Murphy, lock Danny Grewcock, scrum half Matt Dawson, hooker Steve Thompson and prop Matt Stevens – still harboured ambitions of a bench slot in the Test squad.

Lions tours involve a fair amount of myth-making. Any successful trip – and there haven't been many – has to create an aura around itself. One man can do it, or several in the case of the 1971 squad, which was studded with the genius of Gareth, Barry and JPR and overseen by the poetic outsider, Carwyn James. Other tours have had to rely on less celestial beings or more mundane moments, significant nonetheless. The orchestrated punch-up on the 1989 tour to Australia, for example, started by Wales scrum half Robert Jones – one in, all in, triggered by one of the game's more angelic sorts. The tide was on the turn; the Wallabies were on the slide. Eight years later the unforgiving mood was best captured in the image of Wales centre Scott Gibbs dumping the supposedly immovable object, Os du Randt, on his backside. Never mind du Randt, the whole country shook.

The 2005 tourists were still in search of their defining moment. It was up to Woodward to keep pumping out the feel-good vibes. Woodward is good at what he does. He sells a line for all it is worth. His relentlessly positive outlook, backed up

by meticulous planning and attention to detail, is infectious. A few minutes in his company is usually enough to convince you that everything in life is hunky-dory. The players were exposed to it 24/7. They too had the faith.

Woodward's stance at this juncture was that a lot of things were still up for grabs. He was asked if he had selected a dirt-trackers side for the Otago game. 'I've never heard of a dirt-tracking side playing on a Saturday' was his clever response. The reality was different. As it was to turn out, Woodward did still have an open mind on the marginal calls. And one man in particular, Ryan Jones, really was going to make him think again.

The young, long-haired Ospreys back-row forward was in a dreamworld, having been woken in Toronto the Friday before and told to pack his bags for New Zealand. As is the nature of these things, Jones thought at first that it was a wind-up. It wasn't. He was on his way. He didn't waste the opportunity. Reports from training suggested that he was making a mark there too. He was in the side to play in Dunedin. Once again the Lions were favoured to win. It was vital that they did, one week out from the first Test.

Otago, though shorn of some All Blacks, had a stack of players with Super 12 experience. They had a sturdy pack with a pacy back row, and clever half backs in Danny Lee and Nick Evans. Carisbrook – grandly dubbed The House of Pain when in fact it is a ramshackle collection of stands – would be a passionate backdrop. 'Their emphasis will be on the physical nature of things,' said Lions coach Gareth Jenkins. 'They'll come out firing.'

So too would the Lions. Among the half a dozen players still with a real chance of making the Test 22 was Geordan Murphy. The Ireland full back had scored two tries against Taranaki the previous week and offered a creative influence from the rear. 'I'm first and foremost a team man and would hate it if it were ever thought that I'd go out on to a pitch

just for my own agenda,' said Murphy. 'That said, I can't go out and play someone else's game so it's important that I do try to express myself individually. And that's what I've been encouraged to do by the coaches.'

There was one late change to the Lions team, Lewis Moody failing to shake off his knee problem. Simon Easterby stepped up, with Michael Owen – only just back from his round-the-world trip to attend the birth of his second child the previous Monday – coming on to the replacements' bench.

The whole thrust of the Lions victory stemmed from the dominance of their back row, with Jones to the fore. Alongside, Easterby, another of the late arrivals, had a terrific game, while Martyn Williams showed, in the first half in particular, just why he had been so influential for Wales during the Six Nations Championship.

The eye, though, was drawn irresistibly to Jones. The 24-year-old evoked memories of a youthful Lawrence Dallaglio with his surging runs, all-action involvement and teak-hard defence. He had won his first cap only the previous autumn and the height of his ambition for the season had been to cement his place in the Ospreys side. His ball-carrying drives and athletic presence were key features of the game, won by the Lions 30–19.

The Lions flew out of Dunedin on Sunday morning with the greatest of compliments ringing in their ears – abuse. 'They cheat like buggery' was the begrudging assessment from Otago skipper Craig Newby. Ian McGeechan recognised the high praise. 'That's New Zealand parlance for saying that we've come to terms with the breakdown,' said the Lions coach.

And so they appeared to have done. The upshot of another grafting victory at Carisbrook, one laced with longer stretches of sparkle and dominance than had been the norm, was that the mood in the camp was buoyant. The feel-good factor is important. Living cheek by jowl for weeks on end, the last thing you need is an infestation of the glums and glooms.

The impact of a quadruple substitution around the hour mark had a decisive bearing on the outcome. The heavyweight trio of prop Andrew Sheridan, hooker Steve Thompson and lock Danny Grewcock proved an alarming sight for Otago, who wilted badly in the closing stages. The Lions scored ten points in the final quarter and came close to touchdowns on three other occasions, with replacement scrum half Matt Dawson getting the best out of those around him.

The Kiwis were labelling Sir Clive Woodward's squad dull, boring and predictable. Woodward revelled in such comments, for it meant that the first shivers of apprehension were beginning to tingle down spines. That said, the Lions did need to offer a lot more. This game was just an important staging post. They had come off the back of a week of potential hardship and heartache. The defeat by the New Zealand Maori the previous Saturday could well have been followed by setbacks against Wellington and Otago.

The provincial opposition was not as daunting as it once was, given that the majority of the All Black players had been withheld. It was strange that that decision was not greeted locally with the screeches of protest that assailed the Lions ears every time the tourists poked a toe out of line. These parochial, at times arrogant, assumptions might yet have been the undoing of New Zealand. Their coaches were too canny, too worldly-wise, to be suckered into such narrow thinking, but the subconscious of their players was prey to such flights of delusion.

The Lions were capable of a tight, bludgeoning game. But they could score some tries as well. Their scrummage, led by an ever-frisky, ever-resilient Graham Rowntree, had their opponents blowing hard by the final whistle. Will Greenwood marshalled the back line cleverly and gave his best individual performance of the season. His poacher's instincts meant that he was alert to Charlie Hodgson's cross-field punt from a penalty just before half-time, the bounce being kind as Greenwood snatched the ball from between two defenders to touch down.

The Welsh influence on the scoring was marked, wing Shane Williams teeing up his Ospreys mate Jones for his 53rd-minute try, the back-row forward returning the favour a quarter of an hour later when his storming run from a tap penalty created the disarray out of which the wing was able to step inside to score. The Lions defence for the most part held firm, the only notable blemish being the tackles missed in the 33rd minute by Denis Hickie and then Charlie Hodgson to allow scrum half Danny Lee to capitalise on the initial breach by Neil Brew. The Otago centre was a real handful.

Not all was rosy in the Lions ranks. It was painful to watch the sufferings of Gordon D'Arcy in midfield, the Ireland centre so palpably a long way off his best form. The esprit de corps, though, would ensure that D'Arcy did not wallow. 'There is a growing sense of tightness in the squad,' said coach McGeechan. 'The entire squad, midweekers and Test players, has to move on together. They all have to make sure that there's nothing second best about what they're doing.'

What a pity the rallying cry was to fade to a whimper in Invercargill three days later. The Southland fixture was the easiest on the card. New Zealand's southernmost outpost were the whipping boys of the NPC, full of part-timers but with a couple of players of note, such as scrum half Jimmy Cowan and burly No. 8 Paul Miller, who was to leave the field injured before half-time. All the right noises were made about the midweek team sending out the right vibes to their mates who were watching the game back at base in Christchurch. The reality was somewhat different, the Lions scraping home 26–16 in a dreadful match.

The only glimmer – and it was no more than a faint sparkle on an unusually mild winter's night – was in the two-try performance of centre Gavin Henson, the man who had been expected to line up alongside Brian O'Driscoll in midfield for the first Test. Instead Henson had been banished to Invercargill. There was some token tosh pumped out by the Lions about Henson taking the decision on the chin. The reality was different. Sports teams get frightened of their own shadows at times, petrified that an inadvertent comment might give succour to the opposition or fire them up. I've always thought this line of reasoning to be complete twaddle. If athletes at the top of their game need the added motivation of a few paragraphs or a trumped-up headline to really get them in the mood, then it's a wonder they ever get to the top of their game in the first place.

Just tell it as it is. It's better for all concerned. Several Lions players were fed up with having to walk on eggshells when it came to adhering to the party line. They were briefed as to what questions might come up at press conferences, what the angle from within the camp should be. Utter nonsense.

It was only the fine work of one of our colleagues, Dean Wilson of Hayters, that prised the truth from Henson. 'When Clive read out the team I was absolutely devastated,' said Henson. 'It was really hard to take in because I thought I had a chance of making the Test side, so to be told that I wasn't involved came as a shock. I take my game very seriously and this will take a while to get over. I didn't sleep at all well last night. I had a proper chat with Clive and he told me that he doesn't have a problem with the way I'm playing. He said that he just wanted to go with experience for the Test. There are 45 players on tour and the coaches have to make the decisions. I

BELOW Gavin Henson holds off the challenge of Faolua Muliaina (12) to score his second try against Southland. **OVERLEAF** Midweek coach Ian McGeechan looks less than impressed with his side's display against Southland.

understand that. Right now, though, I'm just gutted.'

Henson for all his brash, upfront manner has a less assured, more mellow side, one that is as affected by the slings and arrows as the next man. 'It's a bit like when I got left out of the World Cup,' continued Henson. 'Back then I felt really low. I don't want that to happen again and luckily there are three Tests. You just don't know what will happen. All I can do is try to play well. I have a point to prove. I want to show everyone what I am capable of. At least I have a game straightaway which will help me get it out of my system. It means I can get straight back to what I do best. The worst thing would be to be sitting in a hotel room thinking about it. I really need this game against

Southland and I have to keep playing, try to press for a Test place later in the tour.'

Wilson had simply approached Henson as he came off the training pitch on the eve of the game. The media minders had rounded up the other hacks present and ushered them into a room for the sanitised version of events. Wilson had slipped out to do his job and wasn't noticed, some oversight given that he is dreadlocked and no Kate Moss when it comes to figure.

The evident hurt and emotion told you something far more meaningful than the rubbish put out by the Lions. A Test place really, deeply mattered to Henson as it would to any of the players. Where is the harm in reflecting that? Henson did some talking on the pitch, too, showing his power through the tackle when touching down in the 12th minute, and then again 16 minutes into the second half.

The Lions had made a decent start and were ten points to the good within minutes. And then they went to pieces. There was no fluency, no shape, no precision. It was to be the most dispiriting performance of the tour so far, no tonic whatsoever for those watching from afar in Christchurch. Scrum half Gareth Cooper and hooker Andy Titterrell were substituted just after half-time, a wretched disappointment for the pair of them on their first starts in New Zealand.

Southland flanker Hale T-Pole encapsulated local pride with an all-consuming display and touched down just after half-time to bring the score to 10–10. The Lions had to rely on Henson and the boot of Ronan O'Gara, who finished with 16 points, to see them home. O'Gara's honesty afterwards was refreshing. 'We got a bollocking at half-time and we deserved it,' said the Lions fly half. 'It was frustrating. We felt we were on for a good night after the first ten minutes, but took our foot off the pedal and lost shape. We made the mistake of thinking that they were there for the taking.'

The midweekers trudged back to Christchurch. They had wanted to give a good account of themselves, to press their own claims but also to set the right tone. They had done none of the above. The Test squad would have to do it all themselves.

Cassidy Group, PO Box 2430, Meriden, CV7 7ZX

International Property Developer

Cassidy Group, international property developer based within the heart of **England**.

Projects vary from inner city luxury apartments to exciting mixed use development schemes both in the **U.K** and across **Europe**.

We have offices based across Europe located in the **Channel Islands**, **France**, **Spain** and in **Portugal**

Head Office Contact Details:

Cassidy Group

0044 (0)121 627 5063

info@cassidygroup.com

www.cassidygroup.com

United Kingdom │ Portugal │ France

Channel Islands │ Spain

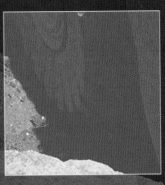

■ The First Test

A fair crack – Clive Woodward had set great store by that philosophy. From the first public statements made many months before the tour, the Lions head coach had stressed time and again that every member of the squad would have a fair and equal opportunity to tilt at the windmill. The sails would spin and spin and it would only be in those closing hours before the first Test that it would be decided who was on board and who was not.

Woodward had grown weary of explaining to people that, yes, he did have separate coaching teams, but, no, that did not mean that he had two fixed playing teams. There was to be no such concept as a Saturday shadow Test team and a midweek dirt-trackers side. There would be a free and easy gangway between the teams. Players would criss and cross. Nothing would be settled. All things were possible. You might argue – and many did – that Woodward ought to have

settled on his chosen men and played them from the start.

As it was, he picked them anyway. When the moment came for announcing the line-up for the first Test, the widespread reaction was that Woodward had chosen the team back home three months earlier. There was nothing wrong with that principle in theory. What was wrong with it was that it cut across almost everything Woodward had been saying throughout the tour.

Jubilant All Blacks celebrate their 21–3 victory over the British and Irish Lions on a drenching night in Christchurch.

Woodward's hard-won reputation was put on the line when he revealed that Jonny Wilkinson would play at inside centre. The England fly half, who had last played in that position for his country in the Grand Slam decider against Wales at Wembley six years previously, was one of eight members of England's World Cup-winning squad to be summoned by Woodward. So much for flux and flow. So much for the Power of Four.

BELOW Josh Lewsey was selected on the wing for the first Test despite having been in menacing form at full back.

The side contained eight Englishmen, four Welshmen and three Irishmen. Scotland were without a representative for the first time in decades. Hooker Gordon Bulloch was mentioned in despatches by Woodward, as was the overlooked quartet of centre Gavin Henson, lock Donncha O'Callaghan and flankers Martyn Williams and Lewis Moody.

There was nothing wrong with Woodward backing those he knew and trusted. It was understandable that he should look to those who had done what so few in the squad had ever done – beaten New Zealand on their own turf. England had won a famous victory in Wellington in June 2003, a significant prelude to their World Cup success only a few months later.

But why the pretence as to how selection might pan out? Why, more critically, not run the team

from the start of the tour? Even those who do know each other need game time on the field. A lack of cohesion had dogged the Lions throughout the provincial matches. The rationale was that all possible combinations had to be looked at.

And yet here we were with a radical revamp of the midfield, with two fly halves, Wilkinson and Stephen Jones, paired together. The radical move won the backing of the man who was to partner Wilkinson in midfield, captain Brian O'Driscoll. 'World class is world class,' said O'Driscoll, who had had just 20 minutes of match practice with Wilkinson, the fly half having switched there for the final quarter against Wellington. 'Jonny inspires confidence in everyone around him. His game is one of the most complete in the world.'

Former Lions centre Jeremy Guscott, in town to promote one of the tour sponsors, Sure for Men, branded the selection 'robotic'. Guscott was disappointed by the seeming lack of flair and flexibility in the line-up. The Lions were going to do it the old England way: bash the opposition up front, kick the corners and then see what happened. It had been a winning formula for England. But this was the Lions. This was supposed to be different.

Woodward opted for Jason Robinson at No. 15, with Josh Lewsey at wing even though he had looked at his most potent running from full back. Robinson, a late arrival on the tour for personal reasons, had not scored a try in 15 games, his longest stretch without a try since switching codes five years earlier. He had been scratchy and patchy, a shadow of the player who had thrilled us all with his outstanding play in Australia four years before.

Perhaps Robinson was still worth a punt, given that he had unique talents, although the likes of Geordan Murphy, who had been in decent nick all tour, might have begged to differ. But why full back? Lewsey had been one of the few players in the entire playing squad who had made the heart leap when he touched the ball. So much else had been flat and disjointed. Why, you might even have found a Kiwi who would have traded Lewsey for one of his or her own. Well, stretching a point perhaps, for the All Blacks were rather tasty themselves in

that department; but the comparison was still valid. Nevertheless Lewsey was consigned to the wing, the idea being that he and Gareth Thomas, would push in from the flanks to squeeze the dangerous New Zealand back line. That was the theory.

There were other potential fault lines in the selection. Robinson was one of six players who had had only one start on New Zealand soil, Wilkinson, Jones, Thomas, hooker Shane Byrne and flanker Neil Back being the others. One start in four weeks. Where was the sharpness going to come from?

Perhaps the only departure from what seemed like a preordained selection lay in the figure of Ryan Jones, the Ospreys back-row forward, who won a spot on the replacements' bench only days after being called onto the tour from North America. Jones had been a real trouper against Otago, full of get-up-and-go. He had clattered forward, taking the game to the opposition. He got the juices flowing.

Woodward did consider a late change of heart over Henson, the centre almost forcing his way onto the bench with his two-try performance against Southland. The Lions head coach decided, though, to stick with his original preferences. A central reason for ditching Henson in favour of Wilkinson was that it was felt that the Wales centre was too quiet, too uncommunicative. Being on the same wavelength was key. O'Driscoll, a robust defender, had missed tackles. He seemed happier with Wilkinson riding shotgun. 'I almost feel that centre is Jonny's better position,' said Woodward. 'I don't think there's a lot of difference between 10 and 12.'

Wilkinson had played his early Test and club rugby at inside centre. 'It doesn't matter what number you're wearing once the game gets going,' said Wilkinson, whose only international outing since the World Cup had been the warm-up match against Argentina. 'I don't even think about whether I'm ready or not. You just go out and play to your instincts. It's my biggest game in that it's my next game.'

There was a solid, some might say lumpy, feel about the pack, with an age-old back-row formation of Richard Hill, Martin Corry and Neil Back. The trio certainly knew their way round a rugby field.

ABOVE Brian O'Driscoll bends to pick a blade of grass as the All Blacks perform the haka. As the ceremony ended, the Lions skipper 'tossed the blade to the winds', believing it to be a mark of respect. It was later suggested that the gesture might have been misinterpreted and led to the controversial tackle on O'Driscoll moments later.

But could they get there quicker than their much younger counterparts? England's Ben Kay was paired with Paul O'Connell in the second row,

another selection that appeared to owe more to faith than form. Kay had not been at full throttle since the World Cup. His game had picked up, but even so there had not been anything conclusive or overpowering about his performances on tour. Andy Robinson had great belief in him as a line-out operator. Hooker Shane Byrne won his spot almost by default, given that England's Steve Thompson had been fallible in his throwing.

New Zealand made five changes to the team that had faced Fiji, with Leon MacDonald making

his All Blacks return after a two-year absence, and lock Chris Jack, prop Carl Hayman, hooker Keven Mealamu and scrum half Justin Marshall all returning to the starting line-up. MacDonald had quit New Zealand after the 2003 World Cup for a spell in Japan, but his form during the 2005 Super 12 and his performance in the New Zealand Maori win over the Lions earned him a recall. MacDonald's inclusion meant that full back Mils Muliaina was dropped to the bench, while Marshall again got the nod over his rival Byron Kelleher.

It was an impressive looking side, stacked with pace and laced with ambition. New Zealand were not going to sit on their haunches and gently probe for openings. They were going to go at the Lions come what may. The Lions knew that. And they were girding themselves for the challenge.

The last verbal skirmishes before the opening match of a series always throw off upbeat vibes. O'Driscoll played the captain's role, stating that he believed his squad were a better outfit than the 2001 Lions. O'Driscoll was quite within his rights to

trumpet the claims of his own men. You would expect nothing less. A less partial view suggested that the 2001 team, with Keith Wood, Richard Hill, Neil Back and Martin Johnson in their pomp, had more certainty to take into a Test match than did Sir Clive Woodward's pack of forwards, if not his entire side.

We harboured hopes for the likes of loose-head prop Gethin Jenkins, lock Paul O'Connell and even hooker Shane Byrne, but we simply did not know if they could scale the heights. O'Connell in particular had to assume the mantle of the warrior. His red shirt had to grow ever larger, his spirit within ever more ferocious and unyielding, if the Lions were to have a chance of trumping New Zealand. O'Connell is a fine player. In Christchurch he had to show that he had the capacity to become a great one.

The pre-match perspective was that all things had to come together if the Lions were to prevail. They had to be at 100 per cent in all that they did. The All Blacks could do the business at 85 per cent. They looked to have half a metre of pace on their opponents all over the field.

Woodward had banked on his team being able to step up to the plate and deliver. He believed that they were both fresher yet harder-honed than their opponents. It would take more than energy and enthusiasm to see off the All Blacks. They may well have been undercooked, their 91-point romp against Fiji no more than a muscle flex, but they dared not renege on their pledge to the All Black legacy. They would fight until they dropped.

There are a lot of platitudes thrown around in the build-up, both sides dancing round the truth for fear of letting slip a trade secret or of unduly goading the opposition. There was a pertinent observation, though, from fly half Stephen Jones as he considered the threat posed by the All Blacks. 'If you are sloppy in any phase, they make you pay,' said Jones. How prophetic.

LEFT Lions physio Phil Pask signals for assistance while chief medic Dr James Robson tends to the downed Brian O'Driscoll in the opening minute of the first Test. The Lions captain's tour was over – he had a dislocated right shoulder.

The Lions had to be exact and exacting. They were to be anything but. They had talked a good game but they were not to play one. Some of their comments were to come back to haunt them. Back had stirred the pot a couple of days before the game, questioning New Zealand's ability to withstand the pressure of expectation. 'There is that question mark hanging over them – can they pull it off?' said Back. 'In the last couple of World Cups they have been the outstanding form team and they've not won it.'

Woodward took pains to praise the mental resilience of his own squad. 'Pressure is a great word because you know some people thrive on it and sometimes people think they thrive on it but when it really comes to it they are not as good as they think,' said the Lions head coach.

New Zealand were happy to confront the intended slights. 'It's a very good thing that there's pressure on us,' said coach Graham Henry. 'That's what comes of rugby being the number one sport in the country. That's what we want. We've addressed the issue with the players. It's important that they are not inhibited by that pressure but feel confident enough to go out there and express themselves.'

There was one other issue to address – the weather. Forecasts were for sub-zero temperatures and snow on the hills round Christchurch. 'It's already in our mindset that we might have to play wet weather rugby,' said New Zealand captain Tana Umaga. 'It looks like it might be a bit of a grind, perhaps not too much of a spectacle.'

It was not to be a grind but, boy, was it to be wet and cold! The day started like many had on the trip – fresh but bright. It was to prove a false dawn, rather like the Lions fiery boasts. The clouds gathered over the distant hills in mid-afternoon, sweeping into town just a few hours before kick-off, drenching the thousands of black-and-red-clad supporters who were all set to party. It made for a dismal backdrop.

RIGHT Referee Joel Jutge sends Lions lock Paul O'Connell to the sin bin in the 12th minute for tackling an All Black from an offside position as New Zealand threatened to score.

It was to get even more depressing for those in red. The storm whipped up by the gods was to be eclipsed by an even more turbulent force within moments of referee Joel Jutge blowing his whistle to start the long-awaited series.

Everyone was on the edge of their seats. The pre-match routines and rituals had got everyone in the mood. The haka, as ever, was great theatre, a spine-tingling moment that is a central part of any Test match involving the All Blacks.

The Lions had prepared their own response, fanning out in a large semicircle round the pitch, with only O'Driscoll and the youngest member of the team, Dwayne Peel, standing out alone. As the

battle cries from the All Blacks faded, O'Driscoll bent down, plucked a blade of grass from the sodden turf and tossed it to the winds.

The gesture was to come under much scrutiny in the days that followed. At the time it seemed no more than a typical Woodward gimmick, a different take on an age-old practice. My own view is that

people get far too het up wondering how to face the haka, worried that the New Zealanders are getting an unfair psychological advantage. Nonsense. All those emotions disappear into the night once that whistle blows. Just enjoy.

Within 40 seconds of the kick-off, the episode took on altogether more sombre overtones. The O'Driscoll–Umaga affair was to hang over the rest of the tour. As the Lions captain went in to drive through a ruck and push back on flanker Jerry Collins, he himself was driven back, first by hooker Keven Mealamu and then, a split second later, by Umaga, each of them lifting one of O'Driscoll's legs and hoisting him into the air. Gravity dictates that what goes up has to come down.

The Lions captain came down with a sickening thud, only a last-ditch push out with his hand preventing him from landing head first on the ground. Play had moved away as the All Blacks came close to scoring in their very first attack. O'Driscoll's tour was over. He had dislocated his shoulder. The physical pain was as nothing to the realisation that all that hard work, all those dreams, all those moments of contemplation had come to nothing. It would be hard to take. In fact, O'Driscoll was not going to take it. Nor were the Lions.

The incident was raised at the post-match press conference. At that point nobody had had a good look at the video footage, Woodward drily noting that the tapes seemed to be taking a long time coming their way. Umaga, meanwhile, mumbled something about there being a few incidents out there that might need further scrutiny.

The dam was about to burst. Within a couple of hours, as the clock moved towards midnight, the British and Irish press were alerted to the fact that Woodward was on his way over to the media hotel for an impromptu press briefing. It took place in the Holiday Inn dining room, with the sound of raucous merriment echoing up from celebrating New Zealand fans down below.

LEFT Recalled All Black full back Leon MacDonald breaks upfield, supported by flanker Richie McCaw and leaving Lions scattered in his wake.

Woodward was fizzing. 'I have no doubt now that Brian was spear-tackled by two New Zealand players,' he said. 'It was a horrendous tackle and Brian is pretty lucky it was not more serious. He could have landed on his neck. The guy was completely defenceless. The ball was long gone. Brian is extremely upset and bitter.'

The tone was set for a week of accusations and counterclaims. The Lions had drawn the attention of citing officer Willem Venter to the incident. Within three hours Venter had made up his mind. He would not be referring the matter to the judicial panel, but he would be asking the disciplinary officer, Australian Terry Willis, to consider whether Lions lock Danny Grewcock had bitten Mealamu.

Uproar. The Lions were incandescent. There was a scheduled press conference at nine o'clock on Sunday morning. O'Driscoll, shoulder in a sling, was there, looking drawn and stunned. As ever, he spoke eloquently. 'There is a huge amount of anger and frustration,' said O'Driscoll. 'I'm disappointed that there's no citing because I feel there's plenty in it. I knew I was in trouble the moment I was up in the air. It was then a question of getting my head out of the way as best I could. It wasn't just a case of being dropped. There was force in it, more malice than is being spoken of from the All Black camp. I'm disappointed too that Tana did not come up as I was being stretchered off. That ought to be a common courtesy.' O'Driscoll could not conceal his hurt. 'It's been hard to keep the tears back,' he said.

The Lions went on the front foot to highlight what they perceived to be the injustice of the matter. A further press conference was called for that evening in Wellington, where video footage was shown for the first time. The Lions felt it proved that the two All Blacks were guilty of dangerous play. In truth, the footage was graphic up to the point when O'Driscoll was tipped over. Then the camera angle changed from close-up to distant and it's impossible to be absolutely sure whether either of the two players deliberately and forcefully drove O'Driscoll into the ground. There is no incontrovertible proof to that end. Venter obviously felt the same way. The Lions did not. 'Brian is not one to exaggerate anything,' said Woodward. 'I'm

RIGHT Lock Ali Williams snaffles a Lions line-out put-in and dives over for the first All Black try of the evening.

just so disappointed that the two players were not even brought in to take questions about it.'

That's a fair point. IRB officials say that a citing officer has to bear in mind the 'red-card test' when deciding whether to cite or not: that is, deem whether the incident might have warranted a red card if it had been spotted by the match officials. That seems a daft and restrictive practice. Umaga

ABOVE Wing Sitiveni Sivivatu, who scored his side's second try shortly after the interval, takes on Lions full back Jason Robinson. **FACING PAGE** Lions stand-off Stephen Jones tries to charge down a kick from his opposite number, Dan Carter.

and Mealamu should have had to explain their actions. I'm sure that they would have said that in the hurly-burly of that frenzied opening they were not aware precisely of what they were doing. Fair enough. At least they would have been made to account for themselves. The case would probably have been dismissed.

As it was the affair was allowed to fester. There was fault on both sides. Umaga, a fundamentally decent bloke, ought to have gone up to O'Driscoll on the field of play. That would have taken so much of the resentment out of the matter. The All Black management ought also to have been more proactive in expressing their sympathy. They,

though, had taken exception to the way in which the Lions had seemingly orchestrated their pained reaction. So they dismissed the matter and threw accusations of foul pay back at the Lions, with coach Graham Henry suggesting that there was 'validity' in the notion that the incident was being overplayed in a bid to distract attention from the abysmal Lions performance. 'The O'Driscoll incident didn't strike me as anything different to any other part of the game, quite frankly,' said Henry, who then drew attention to an alleged stamp by Martin Corry on All Black prop Tony Woodcock.

For their part, the Lions were wrong to pursue the matter through the week, not letting any opportunity slip by to express outrage that Umaga had not apologised. Apologies in sport are a devilishly tricky business. Where do you draw the line? Should Umaga have apologised to O'Driscoll? If so, should Danny Grewcock have apologised to Keven Mealamu for nibbling his finger?

Personally, I'm not fussed either way. Stuff happens on the field. I want stuff to happen on the field. An essential part of rugby's appeal is that it has the capacity for it all going off. It offers many other things, of course – great athleticism, supreme mastery of a variety of skills, drama, excitement, raw power, scintillating pace, all those sorts of things. But it also engages those of us with a lust for the darker side of life because of its clattering collisions and the consequent potential for a spot of mischief. Call me a Neanderthal brute if you like, but a bit of biff never did anyone much harm.

So, if you accept those parameters, then you can't mount the high horse and get all prissy when something untoward does happen. And you certainly don't storm about looking for apologies after the event. Did Neil Back apologise to Joe Worsley for belting him in the mouth in the Premiership final, an incident that cost Back a four-week ban and curtailed his appearances for the

Lions? Maybe he did. Maybe he didn't. It doesn't worry me either way.

What about Martin Johnson and the occasional skirmish he got himself involved in? How did Lions coach Andy Robinson feel about two of his warrior-like Bath fellow-travellers, hooker Graham Dawe and prop Gareth Chilcott, neither of whom favoured the angelic approach? Did they beat their breast three times after each misdemeanour, chant 'mea culpa, mea culpa, mea maxima culpa' and vow to turn the other cheek the next time? Er, no.

There was an email doing the rounds in Wellington during that troubled week, in which it suggested that the French Embassy had been in touch with Buck Shelford to apologise for his nuts being rearranged in Nantes in 1986. It said, too, that the phone of All Black prop Richard Loe had been busy all day as he too made some overdue calls. You get the drift. Awkward business this atonement lark.

The O'Driscoll incident was different, in tone and context. With hindsight, I'm sure Umaga wishes that he had gone over and offered a consolatory pat to his opposite number. No more than that. A gesture. But Umaga should not have been demonised. The sustained and orchestrated campaign by the Lions to put him in the frame did not reflect well on them.

They were absolutely right to raise the matter as a subject fit for possible citing. They had a duty of care to their captain and to the laws of the game. The targeting of Umaga as a real villain was unseemly and unbecoming. To question the integrity and scope of his act of commiseration with O'Driscoll by phone in midweek was beyond the pale. Private conversations should remain private. O'Driscoll deserved better. So too did Umaga.

There was so much else for the Lions to address. There was Grewcock to deal with, an eight-hour disciplinary hearing ending with a two-month ban for the Bath lock. 'I'm glad he's been cited and I'm glad he's been banned,' said Woodward that Sunday evening. 'I'm disappointed in any player that steps over the line. We had spoken to Danny about discipline and he had a good Six Nations. We thought he had learnt his lesson. Obviously it's not happened and he's got what he deserved.'

Grewcock denied the charge. 'I did not bite the player at all,' said the England lock, who had only been on the field six minutes when the incident occurred just into the final quarter.

The lenient sentence suggested judicial officer Terry Willis was not entirely sure what had gone on. 'The judicial officer accepted that Mealamu's fingers inadvertently entered Grewcock's mouth … but rather than removing his fingers in a more conventional way Grewcock bit Mealamu's right finger.' Grewcock had now been suspended for incidents on three visits to New Zealand, having

RIGHT The Lions line out failed to measure up in Christchurch. Here New Zealand's Ali Williams pulls off a steal against Paul O'Connell. **PREVIOUS PAGES** All Black centre Aaron Mauger ploughs through the deluge pursued by Lions Jonny Wilkinson and Shane Horgan.

been sent off in 1998 and banned for six weeks for reckless use of the boot in 2004.

Wales and Toulouse wing Gareth Thomas was to take over as tour captain. At the time of the O'Driscoll incident, Thomas could be seen gesticulating angrily to touch judge Andrew Cole, who was to be the referee for the second Test. 'What I heard as clear as day as Drico's [O'Driscoll's] legs were in the air was the touch judge saying: "Leave him, leave, the ball is gone." Then I heard Brian screaming on the floor.'

The Lions also had to contend with losing two other key players, Wales centre Tom Shanklin giving way to a chronic knee problem, while Richard Hill suffered a 'career-threatening' cruciate knee injury.

Of course, there was one overwhelming matter to address – the complete and utter humbling of the Lions by the All Blacks, the final 21–3 scoreline not reflecting New Zealand's utter domination on an evening of woe. This was the worst Lions performance that many of us had ever seen. There was no cohesion, no shape, no fluency and absolutely no sense of this being 'the best prepared Lions side ever', as head coach Sir Clive Woodward had been billing the 2005 tourists.

The body-numbing deluge that hit Christchurch was supposed to favour the more set-piece-orientated northern hemisphere side. Instead the vile conditions saved the Lions from an even bigger hammering. Given a dry surface, the All Blacks, bristling with intent to attack, would have run in two or three more scores. Only a wonderful try-saving tackle from Jonny Wilkinson on wing Doug Howlett early on and an illegal intervention from lock Paul O'Connell minutes later that led to a yellow card spared the Lions further ignominy on the scoreboard.

There were few redeeming features for the tourists. Replacement back-row forward Ryan Jones was the only Lion to show any sort of gumption and go-forward. Martin Corry, who took over the captaincy, was his usual intractable self, flinty and honest but flailing against a lost cause. Scrum half Dwayne Peel was bright in parts but jerky and error-prone in others. The collapse in form of Jason Robinson was distressing to see. The decision to

pair Stephen Jones and Jonny Wilkinson in midfield showed little yield. There were occasional moments, but in general the kicking from hand was underclubbed and ill-directed.

New Zealand were good value for their scores, lock Ali Williams taking advantage of a line-out cock-up to touch down in the 24th minute, while a superb break and delivery from Tana Umaga teed up wing Sitiveni Sivivatu seven minutes into the second half. All the Lions could summon was a left-footed 56th-minute boot between the sticks from Jonny Wilkinson. The prosaic nature of the lone offering told its own tale.

Woodward's credibility took a real pounding. His rhetoric had built up the Lions, yet it all came tumbling down. Woodward had set great store by the meticulous preparation of the squad, yet the

side looked for long stretches as if they had been cobbled together. Extravagant claims delivered pitiful returns. Woodward wanted his players to be fresh and enthusiastic, but they seemed flat-footed and unfamiliar with each other, a legacy of his decision not to play them together in the build-up.

Bearing in mind that consideration had been given to putting a variety of people in the dock that Sunday, it was surprising that the entire Lions line out was not arraigned on a charge of wholesale incompetence. Coach Andy Robinson, as he himself admitted, ought to have been brought to book. To judge by what happened on the field, the Lions

must have spent more time on preparing their response to the haka than in honing their line out. Ten throws were lost, an indescribably bad return. The fault was far from being Shane Byrne's alone. The hooker did over-egg some throws, but there was simply no co-ordination between jumper, lifters and thrower. The Ali Williams try was a gift.

Amidst all the gloom and introspection, it was easy to overlook the fact that this was a truly accomplished performance from the All Blacks. Given the atrocious conditions, their accuracy and adventure were commendable. New Zealand had long since had style, ambition and thrust behind the scrum. Now we knew that they could slug it out up front, too. There was a masterclass display from their locks, Chris Jack and Ali Williams.

It had been a calamitous weekend for the Lions. They headed to Wellington, wounded in body and in soul.

BELOW With Brian O'Driscoll out of the tour, Clive Woodward needed to appoint a replacment skipper. He turned to the experienced Gareth Thomas of Wales and Toulouse, pictured here at a press conference the day after the first Test.

you WANT FRESH CHALLENGES.

we WORK WITH THE BIGGEST NAMES IN BUSINESS.

together WE'LL SET OURSELVES APART.

From small start-ups to large multinationals, operating in every conceivable sector, the breadth of opportunities we can offer your career is tremendous.

Our clients come to us because they want the best finance and accounting talent. And by perfectly matching their needs and your aspirations, we ensure that's exactly what they get.

So if you're looking for a consultancy that listens to what you want, rather than tells you what you want, it's time you got in contact.

08705 329635

WWW.ROBERTHALF.CO.UK

Robert Half International Inc.

Worldwide Leader in Specialized Consulting & Staffing Services Since 1948

Clive Woodward

The Lions head coach had no option but to admit after the defeat:

■ *'We let a lot of people down – including ourselves. Test losses usually come down to a couple of things – the line out or the scrum. In our case it was the line out. We made a strong line-out selection, but this area was the disappointment. You can't play at this level without guaranteeing about 95 per cent of your own ball. The game just drifted away. We simply did not have enough ball to test the All Blacks defence. But Jonny Wilkinson had an outstanding match, especially in defence. The video made difficult watching. I went into the Test convinced that I had got selection right, but in hindsight I made a couple of errors. I intend to fix those.*

Andy Robinson

The Lions forwards coach sadly confessed:

■ *'We were completely outplayed. We got our line-out communications wrong. We failed to get players in the air, while Ali Williams got in the air effectively on our throws. I accept responsibility. It looked as though they could read our moves before we threw and we could not read their calls.'*

Martin Corry

The England back-row forward, who took over the leadership when O'Driscoll departed, was bitter:

■ *'Throughout the match whatever 15 players we had on the field were under par. We were all poor. It was not a performance of which we can be proud. You want fond memories of big rugby games, but there will be none from this Test. You want to give your best in front of eager fans – and we failed. Mind you, the All Blacks were exceptional.'*

Paul O'Connell

The Ireland lock had this to say:

■ *'There were a few missed calls, then it got worse. All line outs have days like that.'*

Ryan Jones

The Wales No. 8 observed:

■ *'They can't fly out another 22 players. The squad has to front up for the second Test and make it 1–1.'*

BELOW Jonny Wilkinson runs into Richie McCaw and friend.

Graham Henry

The All Black coach, who was in charge of the 2001 Lions, lavished praise on the front five:

■ *'Perhaps we would have won by more if the conditions had been better. But even in the rain the tight five outplayed the Lions and should be given a huge amount of credit. They allowed the loose forwards to function and gave the backs a platform. We played our rugby despite the weather and look forward to expressing ourselves in better conditions later in the series.'*

Steve Hansen

New Zealand's forwards coach was delighted with his speciality:

■ *'It was the best line-out display for two years, both on their ball and ours. We aimed to give them poor quality possession and we achieved just that. We attacked their perceived strength in the tight five. Once you take away a strength, they start questioning themselves. Ali Williams, our try-scoring lock, silenced the doubters and I believe that he will be one of the stars of the series. Our forwards have set down a marker, but we have to repeat this performance in the following Tests.'*

Wayne Smith

The All Black backs coach was full of praise for recalled scrum half Justin Marshall:

■ *'The service he gave was outstanding in the conditions. But all the backs showed remarkable skill levels, given the challenge of rain and wind. We have good backs, whose execution was impressive.'*

Justin Marshall

The New Zealand scrum half was enthusiastic about the performance of his forwards:

■ *'When I made my Test debut ten years ago in Paris, I played behind an absolutely dominant pack and in this Test a new set of forwards laid a fantastic platform. They made my job so much easier. I am thrilled with the way they played. The selectors chose the man to do the job and I thought I did it.'*

Ali Williams

The try-scoring lock was spurred on to a stirring performance by a memory of 2003:

■ *'I remember from two years ago Ben Kay saying how good it felt to beat the All Blacks twice in a row. That was in the back of my mind. It was a good game for me as an individual, but I think that everyone put their hands up and did well.'*

BELOW Ben Kay takes evasive action to avoid Justin Marshall.

Opinion ■ O'Driscoll Incident

Lions one-minute captain Brian O'Driscoll and head coach Clive Woodward seethed with barely suppressed rage after the series began in despair. Insult was added to injury when the accused All Blacks went uninvestigated by the disciplinary authorities. Woodward took the drastic step of summoning the media to view the incident endlessly – as he did when he highlighted on video New Zealand's crossing and obstruction in midfield two years ago.

Clive Woodward

The Lions head coach's view of the episode was:

■ *'In my opinion they were dangerous tackles, but the players concerned do not have to come in and explain – as our Danny Grewcock did. It was a spear tackle. It was foul play. O'Driscoll was injured after just 40 seconds. We are not saying they are guilty, but for the citing officer to ignore the incident is wrong, especially when a player has been so seriously hurt. I disagree that there was no case to answer. It should have gone to the next disciplinary stage. I am disappointed that the right thing has not been done after a high-profile incident in a high-profile game. There has been a suggestion that they took our response to the haka the wrong way. But we took advice from a Maori about how to react, and we believed that we were showing friendship and respect. I hope it's not the case that the New Zealand team was inflamed, because the gesture after the haka was my idea. I can't believe that would be a reason for the tackles. But there is a tendency for New Zealanders not to be cited in their own country.'*

Brian O'Driscoll

Tour captain Brian O'Driscoll was devastated:

■ *'I am absolutely gutted that my tour is over. There is a huge feeling of frustration and anger about the way it*

BELOW Clive Woodward gives his video presentation of the O'Driscoll incident.

happened. I have absolutely no doubt that some sort of spear tackle ended my tour. To have worked so hard for so many years with this outcome for me brings a massive element of disappointment and frustration. There is plenty in that incident. It was completely unnecessary and certainly beyond the laws of the game. Another disappointment was that Umaga did not come up to say anything sympathetic as I was being stretchered off. That should have been a common courtesy from one captain to another, so maybe there was an element of malice in it.

'Fortunately it was not more serious. I knew that I was in trouble the moment I was hoisted in the air, so I concentrated on ensuring that my head did not hit the ground. I have no way of knowing if the tackles were premeditated, but after only a few seconds you can't help feeling more aggrieved. Rugby is a hard, physical game, and the citing commissioner has taken his decision. There were times after the game when I found it hard to keep the tears back, but then I must be thankful for my minute as Lions leader.'

BELOW The injured Brian O'Driscoll, accompanied by Clive Woodward, faces the press the day after the first Test. **FACING PAGE** A thoroughly disconsolate Richard Hill watches the Lions go down at Christchurch, having been forced off injured after only 19 minutes of the match.

Gareth Thomas

The newly appointed replacement Lions tour captain was close to the incident:

■ *'I heard as clear as day the touch judge shouting at the two All Blacks: "Leave him alone, leave him alone – the ball has gone." I saw Brian's legs in the air, and that's why I was enraged and chased the touch judge. I don't think he would have come onto the pitch if he had not seen something. I think that they owe Brian an apology. It has been an ugly weekend.'*

Tana Umaga

The All Black captain was one of the perpetrators of the tackle:

■ *'I don't want to talk about those sort of things.'*

Steve Hansen

The New Zealand forwards coach had this to say:

■ *'I don't want to play silly games. The bottom line is that Brian is injured. That is the disappointing thing, but no one has been cited. We did not want to see Brian out of the series.'*

Woodward revealed that Tom Shanklin and Richard Hill were also out of the tour – Hill with a recurring knee ligament injury that was said to be 'career-threatening'.

A whole new way to fly to Abu Dhabi and beyond.

Etihad Airways.

Etihad Airways offers daily flights from London to Abu Dhabi, a popular destination in its own right and an alternative gateway to Dubai. With our free transfers Dubai is only a short drive by coach - or limousine in Pearl and Diamond Zones.

الإتحاد
ETIHAD
A I R W A Y S
The National Airline of the United Arab Emirates

For further information visit www.etihadairways.com or call 0870 241 7121

5 The Second Test

Where did the Lions go from here? All that talk, all that planning, all those privately nurtured thoughts had blown up in their faces. They had not just been beaten in Christchurch, they had been humiliated. Their line-out play had been a shambles, a stark and illuminating reflection on priorities. You got the sense that they were getting too wound-up, spending too much time trying to finesse the obvious.

The Lions had changed their line-out calls in midweek before the first Test, fearful that New Zealand might have rumbled their codes after the system had had so much exposure during the provincial games. It was a fair enough assumption, but the decision to change was made too late. Hooker Shane Byrne was still mugging up on the new calls just before the Test. Disaster duly ensued.

Small wonder then that at times there appeared to be complete bewilderment among his own players, notably when the ball went straight to All Black lock Ali Williams, who made best use of the gift-wrapped possession by scoring the first try.

The whiff of paranoia is never far distant when it comes to line outs. The 2001 Lions believed that the Wallabies had cracked their calls, an urban myth perhaps, but one that might explain how it was that Justin Harrison managed to steal a crucial ball in the closing stages of the decisive third Test. Not for nothing had the Lions erected security

All Black fly half Dan Carter turns to celebrate, having scored his second try of the second Test at Wellington.

fences round all their training venues, blocking out any snoopers intent on filming.

The Lions did acknowledge the error of their ways. 'In the week before the Test, we thought the All Blacks had cracked our line-out code, so we changed a few things,' said replacement prop Graham Rowntree. 'In hindsight, that was suicide.'

So much for a straightforward, tangible element. That was easy to fix. Ball, throw, jump, catch – these blokes knew how to perform that simple task. They could amend and adjust. But what of morale, that precious self-belief that had taken such a pounding? No one was quite sure how they would react, because the Lions are forever

stepping into uncharted territory. Other international sides can always fall back on previous experience for succour in times of stress. They had been there before, regrouped and come back stronger. That was the theory. The Lions had no past, no reference points. Well, not for this particular group of players. There was one recent landmark that they could tap into and during the week the experience of the 1989 tourists to Australia was thrown into the mix.

Finlay Calder's side had been well and truly beaten in the first Test by the Wallabies, the manner as much as the margin of the 30–12 defeat suggesting that Australia might be set for a series whitewash. Calder even offered to step down from the captaincy in order to get the tour back on the road. His offer was refused. Instead the bugles sounded for a hard core of English players. Rob Andrew, Jeremy Guscott, Mike Teague, Dean Richards, Wade Dooley and Brian Moore rode to the rescue. They got stuck into the Wallabies – literally so, with a mass punch-up setting the tone – and came through 19–12 in the second Test before closing out the series 19–18 in Sydney.

Could Woodward do the same? Had he got the personnel? Would his side go the biff? Intriguing. It soon became apparent that change was in the air. The tourists' side to face Manawatu revealed some interesting developments, notably in the back row. Martin Corry was to start; Neil Back was on the bench. The portents were clear, especially to Corry, who found himself contemplating a huge downturn in fortunes after going from acting Lions captain to dirt-tracking foot soldier.

For the Test back row, therefore, it was likely that Woodward would turn to the gung-ho trio of Lewis Moody, Ryan Jones and Simon Easterby, the latter pair being late additions to the touring party, replacing injured players. 'You don't have to be a brain surgeon to work out the implications of my inclusion,' said Corry, who had been rated by many as one of the few decent performers on a night of hardship and underachievement in Christchurch. 'It's fair to say that Clive is signalling that his initial thoughts might be with Lewis, Ryan and Simon. Good luck to them. The way they have played on this tour, they deserve their chance. I had my

LEFT Martin Corry in action in the 109–6 crushing of Manawatu. His selection for this game suggested that his Test place was on the line after Christchurch. In the event he was not in the starting line-up but made the replacements' bench.

chance and I didn't take it. It's as simple as that. This is right down there with one of the lowest points in my career.'

The composition of the back row indicated a complete sea shift in approach for Woodward, who had put his faith in the England troupers – solid, dependable but short of pace. Woodward had little option but to throw caution to the wind, for the stodgy, measured way had been exposed as grossly inadequate. The Lions had backed themselves into a corner by their own failings. They were set to come out fizzing and fighting.

There was penance to be done for Jason Robinson as well, the England full back getting a much-needed run-out on the wing as he searched for elusive form. Woodward, battling to save credibility for himself and the Lions, stated that some players on view against Manawatu would see action again in the weekend Test match. Wing Shane Williams, full back Geordan Murphy and lock Donncha O'Callaghan would fancy their chances. After putting his players in mothballs prior to the first Test, Woodward had decided that blowing the cobwebs away out on the field was the best policy.

Corry could count himself unlucky in that he had, as ever, done sterling service for club, country and the Lions. He intended to carry on in that vein. 'The worst thing I could do now is wallow in self-pity,' said Corry. 'There's no problem psychologically getting back out there because we are all desperate to atone for Saturday night and get the tour back on track. It's a bit tough physically at the moment because it was a hard game. But I'm not going to make a martyr of myself. I can't afford to take any baggage into this game on Tuesday. If I do get another chance to pull on the Lions shirt in a Test, however slim that chance might seem, from the bench perhaps, than I've got to be ready to give my best. It was not my finest effort on Saturday. Games of that enormity stay with you for the rest of your life, all that regret and disappointment.'

RIGHT Shane Williams, later selected to start the second Test, crosses for the first of his five tries against Manawatu.

The Manawatu game in Palmerston North was to prove cathartic. The Lions managed to flush out a little of the misery caused by the Test defeat with an overwhelming 109–6 victory. There was pace, snap and drive in much of what they did, wing Shane Williams scoring five sparkling tries. There were 17 tries in all, the Lions pushing right to the final whistle in a sustained team display. So much for the upbeat news. The context was that second division Manawatu were by far the worst side that the Lions had faced. The All Blacks they were not.

A side packed with part-timers was bound to tire, but even before fatigue set in, there was a sense

of bullish purpose about the Lions as they looked to atone for the sins of Christchurch. They did that in some style, all the more so considering that they had singularly failed to keep shape in previous games against provincial opposition. Their heads, as well as their hearts, were in gear.

The Lions fell tantalisingly short of several records, ending up a converted try shy of the mark posted against Western Australia in Perth four years earlier, while Shane Williams, with his pace and impish eye for the gap, was one try short of the hauls recorded by David Duckham in 1971 and J.J. Williams three years later in South Africa. This total, though, was a record against a New Zealand side. Had Williams done enough to make the Test team? He had. So too O'Callaghan, while there was also a reprieve for Jason Robinson.

Touring parties latch on to any positives they can. It's a switchback ride out on the road, full of pitfalls and potholes. Everyone knew that Manawatu were no better than an ordinary club side back in the UK. No matter. They could all train with a renewed spring in the step following this game. What, though, was to be the side to carry the battle to the cocksure New Zealanders? We were soon to find out.

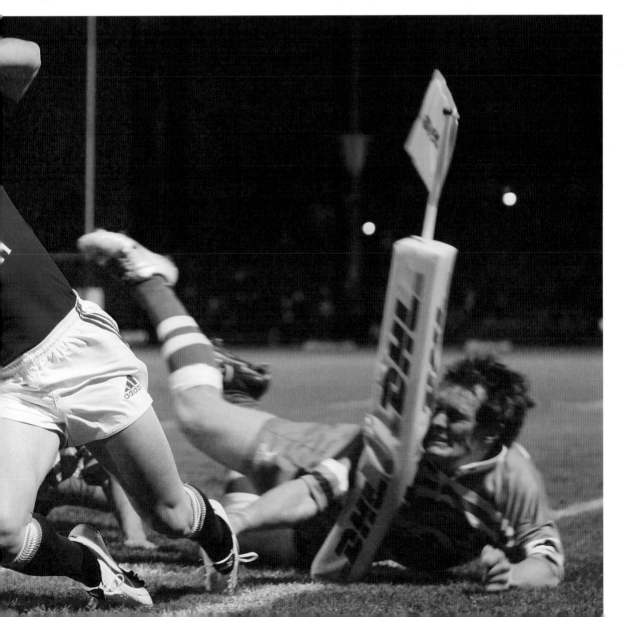

ABOVE Donncha O'Callaghan was teamed with fellow Munsterman Paul O'Connell in the Lions second row for the Wellington Test. **FACING PAGE** Gung-ho England and Leicester flanker Lewis Moody lined up with Ryan Jones and Simon Easterby in the back row as the Lions sought to level the series.

Woodward threw off the shackles of conservatism and went for broke, his team for the face-saving second Test showing 11 changes, seven in personnel and four positional. There was a complete about-turn in selection and strategy. Woodward's standing was on the line, so too that of his team, who were facing a humiliating finale to a flat, disjointed tour.

Woodward was hurting, so too his squad and they had one shot left. 'I've been in corners before, although probably not as tight as this one,' said Woodward. 'There's only one way to come out, and that's fighting. To pick the same team would have sent out the wrong messages to the squad. When you play so poorly, you've got to do something. It's time to shake things up. We've got to put out an attacking team because we've got to win. If you make a mistake, then you've got to fix it quickly. I could have stuck my head in the sand but if you take the pats, then you've got to take the bullets. That said, I've been amazed by the amount of bile and vitriol. I won't forget what some people have said.'

The back row was as expected: Moody aligned with Jones and Easterby. On the wings, the Lions fielded one of the smallest pairings ever seen in Test rugby. Shane Williams got his reward, with Jason Robinson on the other flank. 'I didn't let my head drop when overlooked last week and tried to keep playing with a smile on my face,' said Williams, whose jinking inclinations had caused New Zealand problems before. 'I'm not at all daunted.'

Once again, there were combinations in place who had not played a single moment of match-time rugby together. The distinctly English bias of the previous weekend's formation had given way to a more equitable spread, with Grand Slam-winning Wales now having a significant input across the back line. There were six Welshmen in the starting XV, led by new tour captain Gareth Thomas, who had been chosen in the centre even though he had mainly played wing or full back in recent times. He was partnered by Gavin Henson, contentiously overlooked in Christchurch.

There was a cry of delight from English shire to Barmy Army Wellington base when Josh Lewsey was selected in his most potent position of full back.

Jonny Wilkinson was the preferred choice at fly half even though Woodward had stressed the previous week that it was Stephen Jones who had most impressed him in that position. In the pack O'Callaghan was paired with Munster team-mate Paul O'Connell as the Lions sought a way to find more harmony on their own ball – although O'Callaghan was not renowned as a line-out specialist. Given the Irish alliance, it was ironic that Ireland hooker Shane Byrne, with ten blobs against his name the previous weekend, gave way to England's Steve Thompson, who had had his own demons to contend with when the ball was cocked back in his throwing arm. Woodward had little option, although Scotland's Gordon Bulloch could count himself unlucky.

It was a similar tale in midfield, where an all-Welsh sequence was broken by the choice of Wilkinson over Stephen Jones. 'We've been together a long time now and I'm happy that the units will work,' said Woodward, who had opted for the man he knew best in the number 10 shirt despite the fact that the real form performer on the trip had been Charlie Hodgson. 'Jonny's form in the last couple of games has been tremendous. It was a tough call, though.'

Woodward was under the cosh. He had made such a big play of this being the best prepared Lions squad ever that his words could only come back to haunt him were it to go badly wrong. In Christchurch that is exactly what happened. He had no exit strategy. In many ways, Woodward had bowed to populist picks, a consequence of which was that it would be hard to pillory him if it all fell apart once again at the Westpac on Saturday night.

What was questionable, though, was his switch from a policy of rest to one of opportunity. The team for the first Test did not play for ten days prior to that game even thought many felt they needed a run-out. Here, there were three players – wings Shane Williams and Jason Robinson and lock Donncha O'Callaghan – who had played some part in Tuesday's 109–6 rout of Manawatu. On the bench, the game's most uncomplaining foot soldier, Martin Corry, took his place as cover for the second row as well as the back row after playing a major

part in the previous two games. Woodward was in defiant mood, spiky but determined to bounce back off the ropes. The stakes were high. There was a Test series to save and a reputation to salvage.

Across town, the All Blacks were none too fussed by the routine matter of their opponents' selection. They had decided on three unforced changes themselves, a mark of their confidence and

strength in depth: Rico Gear, Mils Muliaina and Byron Kelleher were good enough to get into most Test sides.

New Zealand were far more put out, and understandably so, by the drawn-out kerfuffle over the O'Driscoll tackle. Umaga's image was dragged back into the spotlight at every opportunity. Ireland coach Eddie O'Sullivan had another dart at it on the Thursday, five days after the incident. The fires of controversy may have died, but O'Sullivan was determined to fan the embers back into life.

O'Sullivan believed that relations between the two camps had been soured. 'There is bad feeling there, no two ways about that,' said O'Sullivan, who revealed that Umaga had finally made contact with his opposite number. 'He commiserated with Brian about being injured as if he had nothing to do with it himself. It's like kicking out the ladder from under someone and then ringing up to commiserate with the fella for having an accident. He's not apologised and I find that upsetting, as does Brian. It's not been handled well and Tana could have gone further with his comments earlier in the week. The incident was not premeditated but it was opportunistic. He knew exactly what he was doing. It's a pity because whatever happens from here on in, this Lions tour will be remembered for this incident. It will colour our memories of it.'

It was strong stuff. It was O'Sullivan's first public take on the incident and he was closer than anyone to his national captain. Even so, the whole thing again smacked of having been too readily aired. As it turned out, it was counterproductive. The All Blacks were rallying behind their captain. A sense of complacency is always a possible danger to any side that convincingly wins the first Test of a series. The repeated slights on Umaga ensured that the All Blacks would be fully focused on the job in hand.

That much had been clear in midweek when Umaga gave his first public press conference. As he came into the room he was flanked by several senior All Blacks. As Umaga was quizzed on the podium afterwards by a gaggle of reporters, burly hooker Anton Oliver stood alongside, arms folded, every gesture a warning not to take liberties. None being taken, Anton, honest.

One for all, and all for one. The message couldn't have been clearer. If the Lions PR machine thought it could pick off the opposition, it had another think coming. 'Tough times don't last,' said Umaga. 'Tough people do.'

Umaga had been demonised, portrayed as brutal and unfeeling. Newspaper leader columns suggested that he had tarnished the image of New Zealand rugby. For some of us, the very notion was poppycock. Umaga is a ferocious competitor, a hard-hitting centre but fundamentally a decent sort. He had had his skirmishes earlier in life, but all that was behind him.

Why, though, had he not gone over to O'Driscoll as he was being loaded onto the stretcher? 'My important role at the time was to keep my own team together,' said Umaga. 'There was a lengthy break and we had to sort out stuff. My allegiance is first and foremost to the All Blacks. I asked about Brian at the post-match and I've tried to make contact. I try not to do these things through the media. I'll maybe have a word with Brian at the right time, and do that man to man. It was an unfortunate incident. I play hard but I try to play as fairly as I can.'

Umaga is a guy who cherishes his privacy. It had been a difficult week. 'It's been disappointing, especially for the team,' said Umaga, who had had to reflect on whether he might find himself holding back the coming weekend. 'That's a question I've had to ask myself. It's something I'm working on intently.' You fancied he wouldn't be tiptoeing across the Wellington turf. As it turned out, he didn't. Nor did his pals in black.

It was a great occasion. There was one achievement that the British and Irish did manage to notch over their hosts – they showed them how to party at the match. New Zealand crowds are notoriously passive. It's not in their nature to let it

FACING PAGE After a week in which he had been the target of vilification in some quarters over his part in the O'Driscoll incident, All Black captain Tana Umaga let his rugby do the talking in front of his home crowd in Wellington. Here he runs in his side's first try in the 18th minute.

all hang out. A few yells for their boys apart, they pay their money and leave their investment at that.

They were wary, though, of the impact the legions of red-shirted fans might have on proceedings. So they revved up their own commitment. Ian McGeechan, a stalwart of so many great Lions tours, said that he had never experienced such a backdrop. Those of us who were at the Gabba on a magical night in 2001 will always resist claims for that occasion being knocked from the top of the podium, but the Westpac experience would be up there jostling for honours. There was noise, there was colour, there was wild hope from one lot and legitimate expectation from the other lot. And then it all kicked off.

There are times in sport when you rub your eyes in disbelief. The Lions themselves had been on their way down the runway tarmac at Heathrow when one of the great sporting comebacks unfolded, Liverpool defying every known convention to come back from the dead and steal the Champions League title from AC Milan. Was Lazarus about to rise again? It took barely 90 seconds for the Lions to suggest that they would be far more involved in this ball game than they had been seven days earlier, captain Gareth Thomas cutting inside a flat-footed defence to touch down. Wilkinson converted and the Lions might have had more on the board but for a reckless flying lunge by Paul O'Connell moments later that cost his side both possession and position. A penalty goal also went begging.

It was a false trail. The Lions did have more to offer. But so too did the All Blacks. And one man in particular, fly half Daniel Carter. Carter scored 33 points, including two fabulous tries. He might have had more. It was his slicing break that set up Umaga for his team's opening try in the 18th minute, a moment of great satisfaction for the All Black captain in front of his home crowd.

LEFT Skipper Gareth Thomas dives between the posts to touch down after only 90 seconds of the second Test, giving Lions fans, already in party mood, something to get really worked up about **(FOLLOWING PAGES)**.

Carter gave one of the most commanding performances ever seen by a Test stand-off. As Wilkinson trudged off around the hour mark, clutching his shoulder, the contrast in fortunes could not have been greater. The baton of sporting immortality was being symbolically passed over. The implicit paradox in that statement only served to emphasise just how fickle fame and fortune can be in the sporting world. The myth refused to crumble. Wilkinson had been feted the length and breadth of England following that drop kick for glory in Sydney. The more he shunned the limelight the more it sought him out.

But Wilkinson then was not the Wilkinson of now. Injury had eroded both self-assurance and timing. Wilkinson was short of match practice. He

looked what he was – a decent player battling to get back to where he once was. He had never made any great claims on his own behalf. It was others who were boosting his standing. He took a knock to his shoulder when trying to tackle first Umaga and then Carter. The 'stingers' affected his left arm. 'Had it been my right arm, I really would have been concerned,' said Wilkinson, who had undergone surgery on that part of his body in an effort to cure the problem.

Ironically, Carter, too, took a knock to his shoulder towards the end of the game, a niggling blow that was to rule him out of the third Test. By then the damage had been well and truly done by the All Blacks. In some ways, Carter is cut from the same stone as Wilkinson. Both are genuinely quiet,

ABOVE The combined efforts of Jonny Wilkinson and Shane Williams are not enough to stop Sitiveni Sivivatu reaching the line for New Zealand's second try of the evening.

modest types who are happier in their own sporting environment than they are in the world of flashbulbs and microphones. They both have a ferocious work ethic as well as childlike delight in what they do. They can tackle, they can pass great distances and they can kick goals.

Thereafter, their paths begin to diverge. Simply put, Carter is the more natural footballer. He has a greater turn of speed, as was shown when he flashed past Henson en route for Umaga's try, and again when he cut inside Lewsey for his own second try. There is a crackle and energy in all he does,

speed of thought in symmetry with physical prowess. Invariably what he wants to happen does happen. He's got the guile and the poise to go with a wonderful array of skills. All this was perfectly encapsulated in his first try just after half-time.

The Lions were still theoretically in the hunt at the interval, only eight points adrift at 21–13. The reality was that there had been a simmering sense of potency in everything that the All Blacks did. The Lions had thrown more at them than they managed in Christchurch. There was much more hiss and spit in the forwards, more precision, too, and a dab more devil behind the scrum even though the supposed Welsh wunderkinds, centre Gavin Henson and wing Shane Williams, came up short. Henson took a bang to the head when flattening Rico Gear with a cover tackle early in the match. He looked out of sorts thereafter, missing tackles. Yet for all the renewed energy of the Lions play, the crunch and vigour of their opening salvoes, it should not mask their grave deficiencies. New Zealand were streets ahead on many counts.

Carter was the epitome of that essential point of difference. There is a swagger and energy in his play that is lacking in the Home Unions' approach. He dares to express himself. By comparison, the game in our parts is cowed, too often frightened of its own shadow.

Carter's try was a gem. A short-side probe opened up a possibility. Carter was on to it. Lewsey pushed up. Most players would have considered chipping the full back. Carter is not most players. Without breaking stride, he simply dabbed the ball past at full pelt. There was so little room to work in. Carter found it. Brilliant. Quite brilliant.

The Lions were not broken, but they were beaten. The forwards, with hooker Steve Thompson and prop Julian White in fiery mood, did make the All Blacks graft for their possession. There were no gift-wrapped goodies on offer. Thompson threw straight, the jumpers leapt and scuffled in the air and everyone was on the same wavelength, although their work at restarts was poor.

Wales No. 8 Ryan Jones clattered about, ably supported by his back-row chums, Simon Easterby and Lewis Moody. Easterby's try in the 66th minute

BELOW The outstanding Richie McCaw, who also made it onto the scoresheet, takes a breather after suffering a nasty gash to the head. **FOLLOWING PAGES** Jono Gibbes, who replaced second-row Chris Jack after 74 minutes, grabs line-out ball for the All Blacks.

ABOVE Tight to the touch line, Dan Carter slots the ball past the advancing Josh Lewsey and chases it down to score his first try of the match. FACING PAGE A dazed-looking Jonny Wilkinson lies prone on the Wellington turf. The Lions fly half was shortly afterwards forced off with an injury to his left arm.

was suitable reward for his efforts. Gareth Thomas led the side with typical gung-ho spirit and set pulses racing with that sensational try-scoring start. But the storm blew itself out. It was a demolition job, with wing Sitiveni Sivivatu and flanker Richie McCaw also scoring as the All Blacks racked up 48

aura. All Black teams used to don their cloak of invincibility with a stern, unforgiving face. Hard men, in dark garb, from the other end of the earth – it was an arresting image. The glower was part of the power.

The All Blacks had changed their ways and changed their style, no longer bullying the opposition into submission but reducing them to quivering wrecks with their irrepressible brand of rugby. They intimidated by the sheer ebullience of their play. The manner of this victory suggested that they would head to the Rugby World Cup in France in two years time as tournament favourites. 'I don't think any side in the world playing well would have been able to live with them,' said Lions captain Brian O'Driscoll afterwards. 'They are certainly a more difficult side to beat than Australia were four years ago with the Lions. They breed on each other's confidence. They're the best I've seen for a long, long time.'

Carter and his pals would no doubt be subjected to more sustained and co-ordinated pressure than the Lions managed in either game. The Lions cracked a few heads and thumped into a few tackles but simply could not hold it all together.

The eye was easily drawn to Carter. However, the significant improvement in All Black play over the previous couple of years had been in the forward pack. In the first Test in Christchurch it had been the line-out duo of Chris Jack and Ali Williams who dismantled Lions hopes. In Wellington it was the all-round footballing

points, a record for New Zealand against the Lions, who managed 18 in reply. It was also a superb exposition of the game's skills. It was time to laud the All Blacks rather than to castigate the Lions.

New Zealand had not just found a new playmaker in Carter. They had rediscovered their excellence of their forwards (led, as ever, by the irrepressible Richie McCaw), their ability to link and support, that invigorated the All Black attack.

Their forwards all wanted to handle. 'None of us grew up dreaming of being a forward,' said Jack, now the most influential second-row in world rugby. 'We wanted to get our mitts on the ball.'

Jack, though, had also done the hard yards. The All Black scrum had improved beyond all recognition, and even though New Zealand were handicapped by the absence through injury of giant tight-head Carl Hayman, they held their own, testimony to the enhanced emphasis put on the set piece since Graham Henry's appointment two years before. Scrum coach Mike Cron had increased their power and prowess. At the 2003 Rugby World Cup the All Blacks were pushing 1200kg on the scrum machine. Now they had ratcheted it up to 2000kg.

New Zealand had long had talent behind the scrum. Now they had a pack taking shape that could consistently deliver ball to make best use of

that potential. 'There were individual performances there from McCaw and half backs Byron Kelleher and Carter that were spectacular,' said Lions coach Gareth Jenkins. 'The side as a whole showed a character, desire and spirit that you might never be able to get into a Lions environment. They were outstanding.'

As with Johnson and England, so with Tana Umaga and this All Black side. Their captain was a rallying point, all the more so after a week of orchestrated mud-slinging. O'Driscoll also revealed that he and Umaga had spoken and resolved their differences. If the two men were now much closer, the evidence from Wellington's Westpac Stadium was that the teams could not be further apart.

BELOW 'It was time to laud the All Blacks rather than to castigate the Lions.' A supporter congratulates All Black coach Graham Henry after New Zealand's breathtaking performance in the second Test in Wellington.

Strength and character don't happen overnight but given time, determination and the right ingredients they emerge.

Brewed longer for a distinctive, full flavour

Nice delivery.

DHL – Official Sponsor of the 2005 New Zealand Lions Series.
Visit us at **www.dhl.com**

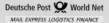

Deutsche Post World Net
MAIL EXPRESS LOGISTICS FINANCE

Clive Woodward

In contrast to the criticism he dished out after the first Test, Sir Clive Woodward this time commended his squad, despite the records that New Zealand amassed and the overwhelming margin of defeat:

■ *'It was a great Test, with a totally different performance from the Lions. I told the players in the dressing room that I was proud of them all and there was nothing more we could have done. No one gave up. We got so much right on the night. I could not ask for any more. The score got away from us, but I deny local suggestions that it was a hiding. Such a description is too harsh. The Lions turned up and played, and I don't feel down. We were opposed by a full-strength and very good New Zealand team. Their backs have always had speed and offload so well. People sometimes underestimate their pack. They are physical, tough and contribute fully to the pace that their game is played at.*

'It has been a successful trip. I would not change anything. I don't regret anything I did. Everybody has enjoyed it and both players and coaches should have learned, but if you judge on the Test series it has not been good.'

Woodward amazed New Zealand observers by stating:

■ *'I would not say that they are a better team than us.'*

Andy Robinson

The Lions forwards coach said:

■*'The forward contest was intense and we gained parity – at times – in the line out and scrum. The critical moments we failed on were the restarts. When we scored points we allowed New Zealand to get straight back into the game, and you can't allow cheap points. We did not put it together for 80 minutes.'*

Gareth Thomas

The replacement Lions tour captain said:

■ *'I doubt whether I will get over the Christchurch defeat because we didn't play. But I'll get over this one easily because there was not one minute when we did not try. To*

me the scoreboard is totally irrelevant. We got great passion and pride from our performance. I concede that we were beaten by the better team, but I deny that the gulf was huge. Still, the All Blacks can mix it with the toughest and run with the fastest. They can attack from anywhere. The forwards can pass and step, then hit where the spaces are. Right now they are the complete team.'*

Steve Thompson

The Lions vice-captain and hooker backed up his leader's assessment:

■ *'There is not a massive difference between the teams. It was about one or two per cent.'*

Brian O'Driscoll

The wounded Lions captain summed up his squad's 2–0-down plight realistically:

■ *'We can't hide from the fact that we will get judged on the result of the Test series. I don't think we clicked as we anticipated, but we can't make excuses about that because that is always the challenge of a Lions tour.'*

Graham Henry

The winning coach could afford to show some magnanimity towards the Lions:

■ *'They played a lot better than in the first Test. They put pressure on us early before we bounced back, improved our defence and played some phenomenal rugby. I don't know if you can play much better than that. Our backs coach, Wayne Smith, and forwards coach, Steve Hansen, can be proud of their units. Both were exceptional. It was all there. It was a top display, wonderfully led by Tana, who was fabulous after putting up with a load of rubbish during the week about the O'Driscoll incident from a person who does not know the game or have a passion for it [a clear reference to Alastair Campbell]. Overall, our rugby reflected the Super 12 style, which has been much criticised in Europe. It's an athletic game and thrives in good conditions, which, fortunately, Wellington provided. It's a great feeling to win in such a manner, showing such class, and I'm sure the country is proud of the team.'*

Henry, though, was irritated by what he considered Lions foul play:

■ *'There were a number of incidents. I don't think that the game is about punching. The game is better than that. The referees and touch judges need to be stricter. There were a number of occasions when things should have been dealt with and more strength shown.'*

Tana Umaga

The winning skipper was not surprised by the Lions sharp start:

■ *'We talked about the Lions beginning with intensity and passion. They had been backed into a corner and had nothing to lose after being talked down between Tests. But they still caught us on the hop with their fighting opening and stretched us. We needed all our composure to come back. But we believed that we had it in us to play great rugby and the ongoing challenge for us is to get better.'*

No Lion tried to 'spin' Dan Carter's tour de force:

Eddie O'Sullivan

The Lions backs coach assessed Carter thus:

■ *'He had a superb game, using the really good service from his pack. His decision-making and control were excellent as he used his options well in a complete display. He was a well-oiled machine.'*

Clive Woodward

The Lions head coach commented:

■ *'He is a special player. He had a wonderful game. He ran so straight. But our Jonny Wilkinson had a tremendous game in attack and defence.'*

Naturally the All Blacks queued up to lavish praise on their hero:

Graham Henry

The All Black coach said:

■ *'He had an exceptional game. He broke the line, scored tries, kicked goals and his defence was excellent. For a 23-year-old his navigation of the ship was outstanding. He was encouraged by Mauger and McCaw.'*

RIGHT The series-winning All Blacks after the game.

Tana Umaga

The New Zealand captain enthused:

■ *'It was great to play alongside such a talent. He runs the show. He is our leader and who knows what he might achieve in the long term.'*

Dan Carter

The man himself, who would miss the final Test injured, reflected on his influential masterclass:

■ *'I'll remember for a long time my great day in the jersey. But full credit to the guys who were working off the ball to create space.'*

A modest man, he continued:

■ *'For my first try I just put the kick through and chased the ball. For the second I was probably a bit greedy. Some of the guys gave me a bit of stick for not passing, but I just put my head down and went for it.*

'In the past we have sometimes followed a winning display with a bad game a week later. So it was a big stepping stone for us to complete a second convincing win. Personally, I am clearly happy with my game on the night. I believe that I was consistent in defence, managed to set up runners outside me and the goal-kicking pleased me. I'm not looking for accolades like world's top stand-off. The bounce of the ball went my way. I'm simply delighted that we cleaned up the series.'

The pull of 400-brake horsepower

You're smiling inside and out

A WORLD APART

The surge of the 4.2
litre supercharged engine

The responsiveness of the Brembo brakes

www.landrover.com

THE RANGE ROVER FOR 2006 Supercharged.

LAND
ROVER

GO BEYOND

Drive responsibly off-road.

▌ **The Third Test**

Back to where it all began, to Auckland and leaden skies, a damp and suitable backdrop. Six weeks earlier there had been rain in the air too, but enough bright interludes to allow for a dash of blue-sky thinking. Gone, all gone. The gloomy reality would resist any makeover. There was to be a lot of self-justification oozing from the Lions camp. There was to be no real acknowledgement of New Zealand's achievement.

Fair enough not to sing their praises too overtly, to boost their already hardened egos. But credit where credit is due. It was not forthcoming and it did the Lions no good to indulge in churlish and ungracious references to the fact that the World Cup is the only barometer worth referring to, the only yardstick by which teams can be evaluated. Even if there is objective truth in what Woodward was saying, it was a bad time to be saying it.

Defeat, of course, is a corrosive wound. The tour still had a week to run and Woodward was intent on keeping spirits high, massaging both mind and body with upbeat talk. It was not until the die was well and truly cast by the week's end that we were to get the benefit of his closing thoughts.

The players knew differently. Players are invariably less interested in dodging issues than are coaches. They see it as it is. These days, regrettably, they are encouraged not to speak their minds, as if

Rodney So'oialo arrives to congratulate his skipper, Tana Umaga, who has just scored in the third Test.

their opinions might somehow reflect badly on others. There is a line to be drawn when it comes to revealing the insider view, and Matt Dawson crossed that line with his warts 'n' all tour diary in 2001. However, the truth will out and should come out, not to satisfy an inquisitive media but so as not to deceive thousands upon thousands of fans who have given their time, their emotion and their money to the cause. They deserve better.

Auckland was awash with red jerseys – soggy red jerseys. The worst weather of the trip hit at the worst possible time, when spirits were low and bodies were flagging. New Zealand is a tough place to tour on so many fronts – climate is one of them. Phil Bennett's 1977 tourists were almost suicidal by the time they finally headed for home, worn down by day after day of miserable weather. The rugby was tough, too. Woodward's men, by comparison, had had it easy, the Christchurch Test apart. To judge by the clouds scudding in over the bay towards their prime-site Hilton Hotel base in the harbour, the Lions would have to tough it out one more time.

Luckily there was a midweek game to both focus minds and divert the blues. The Auckland game was an afterthought to the original schedule and there was not a whimper of protest to be heard now.

Players need games. That is why they flog themselves senseless. They don't put up with all that hardship just to go out and train more. The Lions wanted match time. Some players were seriously short of time out on the paddock, inevitably so in such a large squad. There ought to be no problem with this, just as long as players know the deal when they sign the contract. The likes of hooker Andy Titterrell and scrum half Gareth Cooper had been kicking their heels, logging less then three hours on-field activity apiece. Still, they would have known the score; that they were there as emergency cover.

Woodward was to endure continual criticism for the size of squad he brought. There was nothing wrong in stacking the planes south with so many players – 50, excluding Iain Balshaw, who withdrew on the day the squad congregated. The flaw in his strategy was to give them all a decent crack at a Test

spot. He ought to have been more ruthless in settling on his Test team early on and then allowed the dirt-trackers to do their best to bolster morale with their performances in midweek.

The side coached by Ian McGeechan had done just that, and was ably led in the final three games by Scotland hooker Gordon Bulloch. His selfless commitment was one of the commendable aspects of the trip. Bulloch was desperately unlucky not to be in the Test mix, his time spent guiding the midweek side to an unbeaten return undoubtedly curtailing his opportunities. He was to get his moment of affirmation at the death. A viral ailment having forced Steve Thompson to withdraw on the morning of the final Test, Bulloch was sent on from the bench during the match to replace Shane Byrne. There was no more worthy call to arms.

There were still Test spots up for grabs for the final match at Eden Park, a chance therefore at the same arena for a few contenders to show what they had to offer. Chief among these were wing Mark Cueto, full back Geordan Murphy, lock Simon Shaw and half backs Charlie Hodgson and Matt Dawson. Auckland had eight All Blacks in their ranks but were playing only their second game of the season. It would be no pushover.

The Lions closed the deal 17–13 in front of a capacity crowd of 45,000. The game was like so many on the tour – low on breathtaking, sustained fluency but hard-fought and engaging. Even though the calibre of opposition in midweek had not been of the highest order, to go through unbeaten was laudable. 'I'm very proud of these guys in that they wanted to stand up and be counted,' said McGeechan.

The Lions had to overcome a spirited Auckland side as well as another preening performance from referee Steve Walsh. The New Zealander makes a meal out of so many matters and made so many poor calls in this game, as he had done all tour. He never does the simple thing but looks to make sure that he is noticed. He came close to ruining the match. Quite how he is on the international panel is a mystery.

There was bad blood between the Lions and Walsh, going back to that World Cup bust-up involving Woodward and fitness coach Dave Reddin. The Lions were upset over several incidents on tour. One of the crass calls Walsh made was to penalise lock Ben Kay in the 34th minute for having a dig at centre Sam Tuitupou as he tried to wrestle the ball from the Auckland man following a penalty awarded to the Lions under the posts. Tuitupou took exception and clocked Kay, whose right eye swelled up immediately, forcing him off the field. Injury on top of insult.

Cueto showed well, running hard and true as is his wont. On the stroke of half-time, he did fabulously well to allow a ball to drift across the defender before lancing forward. He then made sufficient ground for Dawson to spin the ball right to Martyn Williams, who plunged over in the corner. There was a typically smart-witted display from Dawson in only his second start on tour. He was busy and canny in all that he did, making best use of a decent supply of ball that came his way. Shaw scrapped hard, as did replacement second-row forward Brent Cockbain. Jason White also played with grit and purpose.

The Lions had to dig deep to fend off an Auckland side that took its time to come to the boil. The Lions led 14–3 at the interval but then had to contend with an Auckland fightback. It was only Ronan O'Gara's 76th-minute penalty that took them clear. Hodgson, as he had been all trip, was shrewd and sharp, drifting through gaps early on, before taking a wallop on his nose that affected his breathing and forced him off midway through the first half. Hodgson had grown in stature and self-belief in New Zealand.

Auckland rallied after the break, centre Ben Atiga looking menacing. It was a sharp break by fly half Tasesa Lavea in the 62nd minute that paved the way for a try by Isa Nacewa. The last quarter was fraught and frenzied; the Lions had enough trust in each other to come through.

The Test squad were in need of every little fillip that they could get their hands on, so this victory was significant in that regard. It was not an earth-shattering landmark, but in the last few days of a deflating tour the pick-me-up tonic was just what the doctor might have ordered.

ABOVE Ben Kay tangles with Auckland centre Sam Tuitupou, an episode that resulted in a black eye for the Lions lock, which ruled him out of the final Test.

Unfortunately the doctor had other things on his mind – sorting out the fit from the fallen. As the injury toll mounted, Woodward decided to delay his team announcement by 24 hours. He also had yet another disciplinary matter to attend to, prop

ABOVE Mark Cueto put in a strong performance against Auckland and cemented a starting slot for the third Test.
FACING PAGE Geordan Murphy was another player to make his Lions Test debut at Eden Park.

Graham Rowntree being cited for a punch in the opening minutes. There was an Auckland name on the charge sheet too, that of Tuitupou, but not, as expected, for leathering Kay. Instead the Auckland centre was brought to book for a stamp on the head of Gordon D'Arcy. He was found guilty and banned for six weeks. Rowntree, after a ridiculously long hearing, was cleared. Once again the whole judicial system seemed flawed and random.

Back in the casualty ward there was a smidgen of long-term good news, the Lions medical staff giving Jonny Wilkinson a clean bill of health even though he had been ruled out of the Auckland Test with a shoulder injury. There had been concerns that Wilkinson might have suffered a career-threatening recurrence of an old problem. Others definitely out of contention for the final Test were centre Gavin Henson ('stinger' neck injury), fly half Charlie Hodgson (concussion), prop Andrew Sheridan (ankle), lock Ben Kay (swollen eye) and centre Ollie Smith (ribs). Simon Shaw and Gordon D'Arcy were later added to that list. Several further players were nursing bumps or ailments. These included captain Gareth Thomas, who had a throat infection, as did flanker Neil Back. Will Greenwood had a sore shoulder, while Shane Horgan required three stitches to a cut in his forehead.

There had been a cloud hanging over Wilkinson. 'I have absolutely no doubt that Jonny is no more vulnerable than any other player to these stinger injuries,' said Lions chief medical officer Dr James Robson. 'He took two knocks to the nerve on Saturday. One cleared within a few seconds, the other has taken longer. He has made fantastic progress and could play next week. He's had three stingers in all in eight weeks, no more than a number of players. He takes full contact in training. He would be found out there if he had any lasting problem.'

If the Lions were bracing themselves for a final tilt at the All Blacks, then Woodward was steeling himself for the criticism that he knew was headed his way. You take the plaudits, you have to expect the brickbats.

There was more salt rubbed into the wounds when All Black forwards coach Steve Hansen upbraided Woodward for using a game plan that was out of step with the modern game. Hansen, who coached Wales from 2002 to 2004, had been expecting a sterner challenge from the Lions and was taken aback by their limited approach.

'The Lions biggest problem was that their game plan was wrong and Clive has to acknowledge that,' said Hansen in midweek, as the All Blacks announced a side for the third Test in Auckland on Saturday initially showing two injury-enforced changes. 'They came with a huge amount of talent but just haven't got the best from them. The strategy needed for today's game has moved on

from that which he used to win the World Cup. He hasn't got a Martin Johnson to drive that sort of game plan through, and he hasn't got a young Neil Back here, he's got an old Neil Back.'

Hansen and Graham Henry both believed that Woodward should have adopted the more expansive style that brought Wales a Grand Slam. 'That was something that Clive failed to recognise,' said Hansen. 'It wasn't by chance that Wales won the Six Nations. They were the best team playing the best rugby.'

It was no surprise to hear Hansen reserve his most stinging observations for the Lions celebrated spin doctor, Alastair Campbell, and his role in the aftermath of the injury to Brian O'Driscoll, after

which All Black captain Tana Umaga had been the target of so much stage-managed criticism.

'Campbell was brought out here to woo New Zealanders and all he's succeeded in doing is hacking us off,' said Hansen. 'It's been counter-productive. The Tana business galvanised the whole team. We're very much like a family in these parts. We're not a big nation and we look out for each other. There's no doubt that it was done to distract from the Lions' own problems, hiding the things that Clive wanted hidden.'

The All Blacks had no intention of easing back on the throttle now that the series had been won. They were without the injured midfield duo of Daniel Carter and Aaron Mauger, who were initially replaced by Leon MacDonald and Conrad Smith. By the following day these plans had undergone further revision, with MacDonald forced to pull out,

BELOW Donncha O'Callaghan makes a break for the All Black line but runs into heavy traffic. **FACING PAGE** Conrad Smith surges home for the first of two All Black tries scored while his skipper and centre partner, Tana Umaga, was in the sin bin.

as well as flanker Richie McCaw. Junior All Black Luke McAlister was drafted in at fly half, with Rodney So'oialo pushed across the back row. Sione Lauaki moved up from the bench.

The Lions made four changes themselves, the back line undergoing a serious revamp; form as much as injury shaped the selection. Wings Jason Robinson and Shane Williams were dropped. There were call-ups for Geordan Murphy and Mark Cueto, the third player from outside the original squad to make it through to the Test side. Will Greenwood lined up at inside centre, with Stephen Jones stepping up to fly half following injuries to Jonny Wilkinson and Gavin Henson. There was one positional change, with Josh Lewsey switching back to wing to accommodate Murphy.

It was ironic that Woodward's last act in rugby union, with Southampton FC looming, was to promote Cueto, a player who had never found favour with him when he was England coach. In another twist Cueto replaced his club captain, Jason Robinson. Cueto, 25, was the first player to be called up from outside the squad, getting an unexpectedly early summons when Iain Balshaw fell crook on the day of assembly. Many felt he should have been there in the first place, having scored 27 tries in 33 matches in the regular season, including eight in the eight games he had played for England since making his debut in the autumn.

'I saw Tuesday as my last chance,' said Cueto. 'In fact, I had no thoughts at all of making the Test team but was just determined to give it one last crack for the season. I've got to try and be as normal as possible on Saturday. If I change anything or get uptight then I'll be destined for a fall. I've got to go out there and do what I know I can do. We've got to show the All Blacks that we've got footballers and game-breakers that can perform just as well as they can. We're playing for pride and for each other.'

ABOVE Lions scrum half Dwayne Peel hands off his All Black opposite number, Byron Kelleher. **FACING PAGE** Lions prop Gethin Jenkins is hauled down within sight of the line by fellow prop Tony Woodcock. **PREVIOUS PAGES** Ali Williams (with scrum cap) is on hand to score as Dwayne Peel fails to gather a grubber behind the try line.

The final day dawned bright and breezy. In Auckland Harbour, former Lions Paul Ackford and Jason Leonard boarded one of the two America's Cup-configured yachts for a quick turn round the bay, the local tourist board doing wonders to put on a good show for the city's many visitors. It was to be less than plain sailing out on the choppy waters, one former Test fly half (Scottish, bespectacled, on radio) revealing his total and utter lack of empathy with the high seas by turning out in civvies and hanging on for dear life as the boats bucked and strained in the tricky conditions.

The Lions had had their fair share of turbulent waters on this trip and were in for another bumpy ride that night. They, at least, were kitted out for the occasion, although they too never quite got to grips with performance under pressure. The tales of each of the three Test matches shared certain key points, even if the narrative of each game had its own distinct quality. For the Lions there was to be no avoiding the fact that when the squeeze came on they crumpled.

Errors, errors, everywhere, at no time more culpably than in the opening stages, at the very moment when the Lions were playing with their dander up. Two tries gifted to a voracious opposition, the scores as well as the initiative handed over to the All Blacks.

There is a simple rule of thumb in international rugby. If you have the ball, then you guard it as if it were an infant wrapped in swaddling clothes. Instead the Lions simply gave up the goodies. They shipped two tries within six minutes at the start and then allowed Rico Gear to round off things with a symbolically easy trot to the line in the very last act of the series, after a wild pass by Will Greenwood.

Under pressure, real or imagined, the Lions had cracked all too easily. Could not they have made it a bit more difficult for an All Blacks side playing below the standard it set in the first two Tests? Let's not cloud this issue with any suggestion of lack of commitment. The Lions gave all that they had to the cause. They toiled and took their bumps and bruises. They were not shirkers, nor were they quitters. Let's not challenge the size of the heart.

But let's scrutinise their ability to think coolly when the heat was at its fiercest. Let's question, too, their aptitude at the highest level. Let's call to account their game intelligence, their street wisdom, especially the need to mould a match at opportune moments.

As they had in Wellington, the Lions set off at a rattling pace. They were two penalty goals to the good within seven minutes, the second of which was awarded for Tana Umaga killing the ball, a deliberate act that earned him a yellow card.

The All Blacks were down to 14 men (as they also later were when Jerry Collins headed to the cooler) and were without their midfield rallying force and captain. It was a golden opportunity. The Lions blew it – big time. Instead of an upsurge in their fortunes, they leaked two tries to Conrad Smith and Ali Williams. The first try saw a defensive cock-up down the narrow side, while a botched dive on the ball by scrum half Dwayne Peel ensured that All Black lock Williams had only a routine lunge and touchdown to perform.

Even though the Lions did manage to rouse themselves for a brief period thereafter, you fancied the die was cast. New Zealand knew that they had

the opposition where they wanted them. The scoreline may have been close at 17–12 until just before half-time, but, as so often, appearance and reality were two different things, as the first of Umaga's two tries, just before the interval, proved.

The Lions had no one of Umaga's stature within their ranks. Brian O'Driscoll had the potential for greatness but was denied the chance to stake a claim due to that highly contentious clean-out tackle by Umaga and his mate. However, O'Driscoll had shown but glimpses on tour of what he had to offer. Umaga delivered on all fronts. He is an inspirational leader and one hell of a player. His tracking runs are of the highest order, as seen when he hit the right support line to take Luke McAlister's inside pass; a catalogue of mistakes – a ball squirting from a scrum, a crunched line out – eventually saw Umaga blast to the line for the second time in the 48th minute. He brought both presence and composure to the New Zealand midfield. The Lions had no one remotely in his class.

The Lions did have their moments. Their line out was productive, delivering Lewis Moody's consolation score, while it was good to see the driving maul make a belated appearance on this trip. Matt Dawson was busy and troublesome. Josh Lewsey had a couple of sharp-heeled runs, yet was also jittery on other occasions. Even the tourists' top men had been afflicted. The Lions finished the game behind their own posts. It was a fitting snapshot for so much of what had gone before.

And that was it – all done and dusted in such a blur. The Lions were on the plane home within 12 hours, sombre, chastened and crestfallen. They knew that they had not given a good account of themselves. They knew that they had had more to offer but simply had not offered it. New Zealand were in cracking good form, to be fair, but they ought to have been tested more. Head coach Woodward could not bring himself to acknowledge their overwhelming superiority.

RIGHT Donncha O'Callaghan celebrates as flanker Lewis Moody (hidden) touches down in the second half for the Lions try following a rolling maul from a line out.

'I ask all New Zealanders to be very reflective,' said Woodward. 'The only time you can judge is when every side arrives at the World Cup, because they have had the same preparation. We've been there, we've done it, we know what it takes. When I see them [New Zealand] winning a World Cup, then it is time to celebrate because it is a tough game – reputations can be destroyed in one game.'

Woodward was to stick to several party lines over the next couple of days. He insisted that he had 'no regrets', and that, the Test results apart, the tour had been successful.

There were no signs of division within the party, of players breaking ranks once they had left camp. Even taking account of the fact that their £20,000 tour contract had a good behaviour clause in it, allowing for disciplinary action for any player bringing the Lions into disrepute, it's fair to say that the players did actually enjoy the experience. They articulated this by referring to the fact that they had made so many good mates. It seemed trite in the context of a hammering in the Test series, so too in the light of the millions spent on the venture. All that cash just so a few players can make friends. The Home Unions as lavish matchmaking agency is not the best advert to parade before the many fans who had shelled out their own money to pursue a similar experience.

The players were not being self-centred. The off-field arrangements had been first rate, with better medical provision than had been the case four years earlier. The excuses for failure had been trimmed to the bone. But the fundamental failing remained. Woodward had not run his men together often enough.

There was some mitigation to hand in that his two very top men, Dallaglio and O'Driscoll, had been felled by injury at the worst possible times. The 2005 Lions never quite had the personnel on paper to send trembles of fear round the rugby world. They would have needed everything in their favour to make it happen. They didn't get it. And so they were doomed. The post-mortem was long and painful, and touched several bases.

Would the Lions ever pass this way again? That was one of the questions that refused to quieten. It was not the loss to New Zealand that so disturbed people as much as the nature of it. A side as potent, as self-assured and as evidently comfortable in each other's on-field company as the All Blacks would probably have beaten any side in the world on home soil.

There was no shame in defeat. But there were grave misgivings about the manner in which the

LEFT Debutant New Zealand stand-off Luke McAlister offloads as he is tackled by Dwayne Peel.

whole operation had been staged, to the point where there were concerns that a Lions trip might not be worth the money, the effort and the subsequent soul-searching.

To my mind, not one syllable of the pre-tour hype was out of place. The concept of a Lions tour ought still to be in rude health. That was the line we took consistently in *The Daily Telegraph* and make no apologies for repeating it. You had to be in either Christchurch or Wellington to fully appreciate the fervour of the following, but to dismiss the hopes and dreams of 15,000 travelling supporters is an insult. There is an allure, charm and excitement about a Lions tour that no other event in rugby union can match.

One of the reasons for the lasting appeal is that tours only take place every four years. Less is more. So, by the time the Lions tour to South Africa in 2009 heaves into view, the feel-bad vibes from this trip will have diminished.

The entire tour to New Zealand, though, had yielded little. Andy Warhol had his 15 minutes of fame. The Lions managed 13 minutes in the spotlight when they ripped into Bay of Plenty in the very first match, scoring three tries in double-quick time, looking slick, co-ordinated and on-message. And that was it. Nine million pounds of preparation distilled into a brief flurry of activity. Harsh, I know. But apart from a heartening gallop from prop Gethin Jenkins against Wellington, some thundering performances from new boy Ryan Jones and several sharp-edged forays from Josh Lewsey, there was little else in the memory bank.

Woodward was pilloried for perceived extravagance. There is nothing wrong in spending money if there is a return on it. It's all relative. Woodward went for gigantism and was obliged to choke on his excesses. If anything, it was hubris that really did for him, a sense that he made too much play of being the biggest and the best. Woodward was hoist by his own claims. If he hadn't talked up

his approach, then the barbs would not have stung as much.

The Lions will survive this. It's time also to highlight one central misconception. Four times one does not equal four in Lions terms. New Zealanders expected the team to be the sum of their parts; that they would somehow be four times stronger than England, Wales, Ireland or Scotland. They rarely are; not unless there are at least three truly world-class players in each country. If

RIGHT Scottish Lions fans go wild as Gordon Bulloch leaves the bench in the 70th minute to become the first Scottish player to receive a Test cap on the 2005 tour.

anything, the Lions are weaker than each individual country in that they are searching for pattern and understanding. Usually that evolves. With Woodward's Lions it did not. The fundamental and enduring appeal of the Lions is that it is so bloody difficult. That is why it will happen again.

There were lessons to take on board. The 67-point differential between the teams is a damning ledger, so too the 12–3 try tally. One side played rugby, the other clung on for dear life.

The Lions left behind a sense of emptiness, of anticlimax, even of bewilderment. All that time, all that effort, all that money – and so little to show. They left behind no footprints in the New Zealand soil. However, there were scorch marks across the Christchurch, Wellington and Auckland turf, all black-edged. There was no doubt that New Zealand had played the game at a different pace to the Home Unions. Only Wales had begun to understand that if defence had been the ogre of the

age, then a new era of attacking enlightenment was about to dawn.

England had won the World Cup through their ferocious will power, a resolute game plan and Jonny's boot. Sir Clive Woodward thought he could do the same with the Lions. His selection for the first Test was a blunder, one that put the Lions on the slide.

Teams that score tries will scoop the prizes. England, Ireland and Scotland needed to take note. Wales already had. Woodward used to think that way himself. Caution is the snare that can trap every man. Woodward failed to dare.

You couldn't help feeling that one of the things that did for Woodward was the fact that he wanted to do everything that Graham Henry had not done as Lions coach four years earlier in Australia. Bigger squad, no split between midweek and Saturday teams, and a central base. Woodward ought to have adapted his plans as he went along.

Woodward's time in rugby was up. There was a sense that he had become too corporate, too overblown and too brand-conscious. Woodward got praised too much for England winning the World Cup and bore too much of the brunt for the Lions losing in New Zealand. In short, too much centred around him.

Listen instead to Ireland lock Paul O'Connell, who took over the captaincy in the final Test when an ailing Gareth Thomas was substituted. 'I think we have to take collective responsibility,' said the Munsterman. 'There were mistakes made but at the same time I think Clive needed players to produce the goods, and myself and other guys haven't done that. Maybe you can point the finger at the coaching staff but we are all experienced players and not one of us can hold our hands up and say we've had good tours. We had no real stand-out players. A lot of us just didn't bring our A games with us.'

LEFT Rico Gear chips over Josh Lewsey and sets off to score with the final play of the series. **RIGHT** New Zealand All Black captain Tana Umaga raises aloft the trophy for the winners of the DHL Lions Series 2005.

We had high hopes of O'Connell. We wanted him to be the next Martin Johnson. In the end, he wasn't even the current Paul O'Connell. O'Connell's blunt and honest assessment is one that should head any tour appraisal. The coaches ought to have got more from their men, and Woodward ought to have approached key parts of the trip differently.

Instead of searing honesty, though, we had some bizarre reflections. Woodward was already talking in curious terms on Saturday night of expanding the schedules; to bring more players, more coaches, and to perhaps play Tuesday and Thursday as well as Saturday. 'I'm flabbergasted,' said All Black coach Graham Henry.

So were a lot of us. Woodward also made claim that the media failed to get the best out of Campbell, a quite ludicrous statement. Campbell himself stated as much in a *Sunday Times* interview.

God spare us. There was a storm-in-a-teacup row that weekend over Campbell's involvement in a picture taken mid-tour of Gavin Henson, in which the Wales centre was shown in seemingly convivial mood with Woodward despite the fact that he had just been left out of the first Test. I have no beef with Campbell stage-managing pictures. That's his job. It's up to the media to interpret them correctly.

I take issue, though, with his assertion that he was ready to give ideas and that we had all missed a trick in not seeking him out. Given that Campbell was back in the UK on pre-arranged business mid-tour, given that the apparatus he had put in place for media operations was effectively dismantled while he was away because it was causing so much friction and bother, given that he admitted himself that he knew bugger all about rugby union prior to departure, then I think the hacks got it right.

I had no problem with his initial appointment. However, I firmly believe that, rather like the Lions, he was not all he was cracked up to be. He was a pleasant enough bloke but, in short, he did not adapt to circumstance. He remained as he was at Westminster, a rather shadowy figure. Even if he wasn't up to tricks, everyone thought he was.

The New Zealand public thought he was up to no good, spinning truth and manipulating the message. Well, there was one truth that simply could not be distorted. The Lions were beaten by an overwhelmingly better side, but they ought to have been that much better themselves.

Clive Woodward

Sir Clive, who bowed out of rugby coaching after seven years with England and a year planning this Lions trip, said:

■ *'I was realistic when I took on the job. We had lost nine times in ten tours. Now it's ten from eleven. I was under no illusions. We have to keep things in perspective and take a balanced view. We've lost and that's how I will be judged. But I know that every player enjoyed his tour. They have been fantastic ambassadors. I still don't think that there is a gulf between the two teams. There is no difference between the north and the south if you have a level playing field. In this match we had combinations who had never played alongside each other. In the end we ran out of players, after losing key men early on the tour, like Brian O'Driscoll and Lawrence Dallaglio. The only time you can judge teams is at World Cups when everyone arrives with the same preparation and at full strength.'*

Andy Robinson

The Lions forwards coach admitted that the Lions had had shortcomings and had paid for them:

■ *'We were heavily punished for our errors and turnovers in all Tests. We lost line outs and restarts. For New Zealand to lose their captain to the sin bin and immediately turn a 6–0 score into 14–6 means that we have got to look at our mistakes. We lacked efficiency at the set piece and they killed us. The difference in efficient finishing was highlighted by the 5–1 try count.'*

Eddie O'Sullivan

The Lions backs coach explained:

■ *'Three of the New Zealand tries came from mismatches in defensive situations. Their execution rate was very high*

BELOW Lions coaches Woodward and Robinson try to rally their downcast troops at the end of the third Test.

and they do not need to be asked twice to score. There were also differences in individual skills.'

Gareth Thomas

While applauding New Zealand, the replacement tour skipper also pointed up his side's resilience:

■ *'It's been a difficult series, but at no point did we give up. In Wellington and in Auckland we let the All Blacks back into the game after taking early leads. If you concede turnovers to New Zealand you get punished. They take their*

try chances. They are quality. They showed us how to win in clinical fashion.'

Josh Lewsey

The Lions wing conceded:

■ *'We are very disappointed. They were a much better team. They gave us a lesson how to play attacking football. We English players have to take it back if we are to have any chance of retaining the World Cup in 2007. We were ashamed of our play in the first Test in Christchurch. We gave it everything in the next two, but were still not good enough. We tried to play with the ball in hand, but that takes so much time to develop. The big disappointment is that there are so many talented players in this squad who do not deserve to go down in rugby history as 3–0 losers. But fair enough. You have to hold up your hands and admit their superiority.'*

Stephen Jones

The Lions fly half had this to say:

■ *'The rugby side was frustrating because I think we could have played better. But you have to give New Zealand credit. The difference was their dynamism at the breakdown.'*

Lewis Moody

Reflecting on the tour, the Lions flanker remarked:

■ *'In seven weeks we hoped to find the right mixture to take on the best in the world. I have enjoyed every minute of the tour. It is a shame we could not deliver on the pitch. At the end of the day, they were a better team.'*

Graham Henry

The All Black coach gave his view on the Test, the tour and the Lions:

■ *'It's very pleasing to win the series 3–0. We played some stylish rugby, especially in the first two Tests. Even though we scored five tries to one in this final game, it was not as good a game as the opening two matches. The tour has been superb for New Zealand as a country. The Lions supporters have been superb, but like the team and management they will be disappointed about the results. I have to pay tribute to two men at contrasting stages of their*

LEFT New Zealand's Byron Kelleher whips the ball away under the gaze of Rodney So'oialo and a predatory Lewis Moody.

RIGHT Debutant All Black Luke McAlister had a big act to follow replacing the injured Dan Carter. However, his assured display in the number 10 shirt underlined the strength in depth of New Zealand rugby.

careers. In his 82nd Test, our scrum half Justin Marshall signed off his All Blacks career by coming on as a sub with some style. And in his first run-out in the black jersey Luke McAlister gave a special display of control and goal-kicking in his debut Test. Luke normally plays at centre and it was satisfying for the coaching team to watch him adapt so successfully to his role when he was following Daniel Carter's amazing display in the second Test in Wellington. It's great for his confidence and our future knowing that we have such a talent in our squad. And our captain, Tana Umaga, was the player of the night and the series.

'Even though the Lions lost, they must survive. The Lions brand is special. Every time they tour it's a major occasion and they have had some great teams over the years. From my time as coach of the 2001 Lions in Australia I still have a bit of Lion in me. It is essential that they continue. Ask the players in Britain and Ireland. They see a Lions shirt as the peak of their careers. They would be disappointed if that goal was taken away.'

Wayne Smith
The All Black backs coach remarked:
■ *'We kicked more than usual, but we reacted to what we saw in the opposition. The communication by the backs was wonderful.'*

Tana Umaga
Meanwhile the captain paid tribute to his coaches:
■ *'They worked incredibly hard in ensuring that we were able to deliver our best rugby when it mattered. And the players around me in all the Tests withstood the pressure and expectation that built up as the series loomed. We became tighter as a unit and the new members who came in after selection decisions and injuries did not look out of place. We have great depth. We studied the Lions and combated their game plan. When I was in the sin bin, the boys focused. A yellow can work two ways. You can leak points or react strongly to adversity. The boys scored 14 points while I was on the touch line. Perhaps they don't need me as much as I was starting to believe.'*

Umaga agreed with Henry's view of the Lions as an attraction:
■ *'For the All Blacks playing against them is the next best thing to competing in a World Cup – above the Tri-Nations.'*

Justin Marshall
The veteran scrum half observed:
■ *'They came here expecting to control the scrum and line out, but at the set piece we were a lot more physical than they would have planned for.'*

**European
Growth Fund**

**Specialist
Investment Group**

**UK Special
Situations Fund**

**Best Unit
Trust Group**

**Best UK
Funds Group**

**Europe Ex UK –
Philip Wolstencroft – Winner**

Skill, determination and teamwork.
That's what brings home *the trophies*.

**Fund Management
Group**

Best UK Growth Fund

**Best Equity
Group – Large**

Best European Fund

**People's Choice Best Fund
Provider Runner-up**

**Best UK Equity
Group – Large**

**Best UK
Equity Growth Group**

L IKE LIONS we hunt in packs. Working with cold-eyed determination as a team. Pouncing only when the moment is exactly right. But unlike Lions we stalk the investment world, chasing after Profits not rugby balls. A sport that has brought us thirteen awards in the last twelve months. (There are no prizes for a 'decent try' in our game.)

Please remember that past performance should not be seen as a guide to future performance. The value of an investment and any income from it can fall as well as rise as a result of market and currency fluctuations and you may not get back the amount originally invested.

Come hunting with a different animal altogether. See the contact details below.

*Fig.1 A typical
PROFIT*

ARTEMIS
The PROFIT Hunter

Telephone: *0800 092 2051*
E-mail: *investorsupport@artemisfunds.com*
Web: *www.artemisonline.co.uk*

Postscript ■ The Life of Brian

BY BRENDAN GALLAGHER

Rarely has a season promised so much yet delivered so little. Lions captain Brian O'Driscoll has been touched with luck, as well as genius, throughout his meteoric career, but the former deserted him in 2005 and the latter appeared only sporadically. It was as hard and grimy a shift at the coalface as he is ever likely to experience, and when he finally clocked off after just 40 seconds of the first Test in Christchurch he would have uttered a good riddance to the toughest season of his life.

'Yes, without doubt the hardest season of my life,' admitted O'Driscoll as he finally boarded the plane home from New Zealand. 'You can plot and plan all you want, but sport rarely grants you a clear run at anything. It's been a season of failure and it hurts, but I am still only 26 and there is time enough to make dreams come true.'

It all started so well – Ireland in great form in autumn 2004 with important wins over Tri-Nations champions South Africa and over Argentina, who arrived in Dublin fresh from an historic win over a full-strength France in Marseilles. And it was going swimmingly with Leinster as well – only the third team to qualify for the Heineken Cup quarter-finals with a 100 per cent pool record.

And casting its apparently benevolent light over everything was the pot of gold at the end of the tunnel – the Lions captaincy in New Zealand – which also appeared a strong possibility. He wanted that badly, and after an outstanding tour as a player in Australia four years previously and a successful stint as Ireland's leader, the captaincy was surely his to lose. Life was sweet.

And then, gradually, brick by brick, the wall came crashing down, underlining, yet again, that the life of a sportsman is a precarious one.

Something wasn't quite right with Ireland after Christmas. They had lost their autumn zip and were struggling to live up to their Grand Slam expectations. Worse still for O'Driscoll, he tore his hamstring in the last minute of the opening game against Italy and found himself banished to the ice chambers of Spala in an attempt to regain fitness.

He did, and scored a cracking try to clinch victory over England on his comeback. But still Ireland weren't firing and were found wanting in their next game – at home to France – when their Grand Slam dreams became the stuff of nightmares. A week later Wales rubbed salt into Irish wounds by claiming the ultimate prize themselves, against O'Driscoll's men at a sweltering Millennium Stadium.

A couple of weeks later Leinster went crashing out of the Heineken Cup, outclassed by Leicester at a packed Lansdowne Road. Rancour was in the air, and the atmosphere was scarcely improved when Leinster coach Declan Kidney announced he was off back to his native Munster.

But there was still the Lions. His appointment as captain on 11 April 2005 was a proud moment and was widely applauded. Things would surely start looking up.

Wrong – well, ultimately wrong. For a while hope was in the air and he went about his captaincy duties with brisk purpose. But it all started to go pear-shaped after just 15 minutes of the opening game in New Zealand, against Bay of Plenty in Rotorua. Three sparkling tries, but then Lawrence Dallaglio departed with a badly damaged ankle and you could see O'Driscoll's head bow a little. Not particularly close before the tour, the two players had immediately struck up a strong friendship, and it was clear to one and all that Dallaglio would be O'Driscoll's right-hand man and pack leader. Now, at one fell swoop, the Lions had been dealt a massive blow and O'Driscoll left a little adrift and disorientated. There are those who would argue that Dallaglio's injury was the key moment of the entire tour.

The caravan moved on. Taranaki was positive enough, but the Lions quickly underwent a reality check when they encountered a pumped-up Maori who defeated them more comfortably in Hamilton than the 19–13 scoreline would suggest. O'Driscoll scampered in for one of the tour's best tries, but it was no consolation, and he, like others, was angry at a couple of missed tackles and at the lack of physicality shown by the Lions at the breakdown.

Four days later the shadow Test team, as we later realised it was, performed fitfully in defeating an understrength Wellington 23–6. The home coach, John Plumtree, ventured the opinion that the Blacks would have put 50 or 60 points on his team – an absolutely spot-on estimation and form line, as the Tests were soon to prove.

The writing was on the wall, but O'Driscoll attempted to rally the troops all week in Christchurch. Much would depend upon him raising his game and leading by example, but in what became the cause célèbre of the tour his participation in the Tests

BELOW Brian O'Driscoll leads the Lions out for the first Test at Christchurch.

was over after just 40 seconds, courtesy of Keven Mealamu and Tana Umaga.

Acres of newsprint and comment followed, some of it fatuous; but to suggest that nothing untoward happened and this wasn't a genuine story worth investigating was clearly nonsense. When New Zealand's staunchly patriotic national paper the *Herald* ripped into the All Blacks and Umaga as it did on the Tuesday following the incident, it was clear that it wasn't only the Lions who were unhappy about the entire scenario.

Eventually Umaga contacted O'Driscoll on the Wednesday night to enquire after his health. They spoke privately about the episode and agreed that neither would repeat what was said. There they chose to end the matter, though nothing either captain could do would prevent it being the pre-eminent story of the tour.

As for the series itself and the 3–0 whitewash: 'We just didn't click like we should have done,' admitted O'Driscoll. 'And that is disappointing, frustrating and something of a mystery to me because we were a very happy group and we trained well. Losing Lawrence was a huge blow, but it was undoubtedly a lost opportunity, because whenever you get picked for the Lions, you are expected to go down and win the Test series, whether it is against New Zealand, Australia or South Africa.

'Tours are always judged on their success, and this one will go down as a disappointment, but I have felt that on my previous Lions experience four years ago, the enjoyment factor of this tour has been far more significant than then. But it is all about winning in the end, and you just have to accept it.

'When you look at the clinical way in which the All Blacks played, I don't think any side in the world playing well would have been able to live with them,' he added.

'Comparing it to four years ago, they are certainly a more difficult side to beat than Australia were. New Zealand were super. They have moved on at an extraordinary pace since the World Cup and if nothing else we now know exactly what we all have to do if we are going to match them in France in two years' time.'

Postscript ■ Graham Henry

WITH ALASTAIR HIGNELL

That was a very emphatic series win. You must be as happy about the manner of the series victory as about the size of the victories.

■ *I think the guys have performed really well. They played in awful conditions in Christchurch and ideal conditions in Wellington and they've handled those pretty well. There's a lot of intrinsic motivation in the squad with guys wanting to play well as individuals and as a group. There's a lot of cross-motivation between individuals. They spend a lot of time encouraging each other so I'm basically unemployed.*

You were with the Lions in Australia, lost 2–1. How much do you relate to Sir Clive Woodward's plight in New Zealand?

■ *Oh yeah, I've got some memories of that. I thought we played some excellent football on that, but we just fell apart really. We should have won the second Test … If we'd done that it would have been a very, very fine memory. But we had so many injuries – only eight guys were fit to train on the Wednesday before the final Test in Sydney. And they still played pretty well. They had a lot of heart. I have enormous respect for what the guys did on that tour. They didn't quite make the grade in the finish, but the vast majority of individuals who made up that tour were very committed, wanted to do the job, and were great to work with.*

Lions tours always come at the end of the northern hemisphere season, and you've mentioned the problems you had with injuries in 2001. Sides like the All Blacks are developing constantly. In the professional era, when the Lions only have six weeks to get together, have they got any chance in the future of winning a Test or even winning a series?

■ *Oh yeah, I think so. They pick from four countries … and have a lot of quality players to choose from, and they are looked after – particularly on this tour. I guess it's a question of getting that balance right, which is always a difficult thing. How much they play together and how much you rest them and to play against quality opposition … I think you need to be exposed to get better … This Lions team – with all due respect to the provincial sides they've encountered – haven't faced sides of real quality, except for the New Zealand Maori side in the third match at Hamilton, and I think you need to play sides of real quality to progress … So I think one of the things I've learned from this tour is you need to play the Super 12 sides – or in the future the Super*

BELOW Graham Henry's Player of the Series, All Black captain Tana Umaga, piles through Ryan Jones's tackle to score in the third Test at Auckland.

14 sides – so that you get top opposition so you know where you're at before you go into the Test matches.

How surprised are you that this Lions side hasn't put together any memorable rugby on the tour?

■ *Very surprised. There's always a bit of a Lion in you when you've been involved on a tour. There's still a bit of Lion in me. I have huge respect for the brand, a huge respect for the players who play in the team and know that it is the ultimate in their rugby careers. So even now I'm the opposition coach, I can relate to what's going on and I've got huge respect for what it all means. So I am disappointed that they haven't produced the rugby they were capable of.*

How would you characterise this All Black side?

■ *Enjoyed selves, enjoyed playing, expressed enjoyment on the field. They've played with discipline, and set high standards. They are developing as a rugby team. We have yet to see how good they can be, but I am hopeful we are on the right track. We witnessed outstanding displays from Dan Carter and Richie McCaw in the first two Tests, we successfully blooded youngsters like Luke McAlister in the third, but if I had to pick a Player of the Series, it would be Tana Umaga. I thought his contribution was astronomical. He was able to play so well because the guys round him have started taking on leadership. That means he can be more relaxed mentally while physically he's shown he's in great shape.*

England won the World Cup playing a forward-based, risk-averse type of rugby, underpinned by superlative goal-kicking. How much do you think the game has moved on?

■ *Hugely. I think you need a multi-dimensional game. I don't think you can pick a great big forward pack and a kicking 9 and 10 and win rugby games unless you're playing in a blizzard. No disrespect for the game in the past. It was very successful, but I think our style is good for the broadcasters, it's good for the fans, and it's good for the players because it means they enjoy the game a lot more, and it's more stimulating and demanding on coaches.*

Do you think the Lions underestimated New Zealand?

■ *I wouldn't have thought so. I know they made a point of underlining just how successful past All Blacks sides have*

been against the Lions, so I don't think there was any chance that Sir Clive underestimated the task in front of his team.

Were the Lions poor or the All Blacks very good?

■ *I thought the All Blacks played quality rugby. I thought the Lions played soundly. I thought we had more game-breakers than they had. I think they came over thinking a particular team was going to win the first Test and I think that was a mistake. But I know from my experience as the Lions coach last time around that the Lions players would have given everything to make sure they were successful on this tour. It just didn't happen. They gave it their best shot, but they were up against a better team. We outplayed them. That's the way of the world. Somebody's got to lose in a game of rugby.*

Can the Lions compete in the professional world? If they can't win with so much money and so many resources thrown into the effort, how will they be able to survive in the future?

■ *Most definitely. They must survive. I think the Lions brand is something special, and every time they tour it's a major occasion. They've had some great teams over the years, and I know the players in the four Home Unions regard it as the peak of their careers to be selected for the Lions. It would be awful to have that taken away from them. I think it's essential that the Lions continue.*

When I spoke to you at the start of the season, you said this tour was the most important thing outside of the World Cup for New Zealand rugby. Now, after thrashing the Lions 3–0, the papers are writing you up as favourites – some as far as calling you guaranteed winners – at the next World Cup. What's your reaction to those claims?

■ *We can't control what people say about us or write about us. What is fair to say is that we are a developing rugby team, but there is a lot of water to run under the bridge over the next two years. I know, because I've been in this game long enough, that you have both ups and downs. I fully expect us to come in for a few downs before the next World Cup.*

Clive Woodward says that although this All Black side is very good, no one should get carried away until they've seen how they perform in a World Cup. What's your take on that?

■ *I think that's a very good camouflage. You can spin it any way you like. But what do you do? Are you supposed to not win campaigns leading up to World Cups? The idea's ridiculous, not worth commenting on really.*

Clive Woodward has gone on record saying he would if anything have brought a bigger squad. What are your thoughts on that?

■ *I assume that's in jest. If it's not, I'm flabbergasted.*

Now Sir Clive is leaving rugby, the verbal jousting between you two is likely to end. Will you miss him?

■ *I think it's been a positive rivalry. For a long time I didn't think of it as a rivalry between two individuals, but people have painted it that way. I wish him well in pastures new.*

You received a lot of stick as losing Lions coach in 2001. Do you expect Sir Clive to come in for the same sort of criticism?

■ *2001 was a blessing. I wouldn't be where I am today if it wasn't for 2001. The ribbing I got pushed me back to New Zealand more quickly than I might have chosen, but it's*

worked out pretty well. It was a great series, 2001. We scored seven tries apiece, but I won't dwell on that. We should have won the series. We played great rugby then. Of course I have no idea what the try count has been against the Lions. I have lost count.

Did the Lions let themselves down?

■ *I think they did their best, but the All Blacks played some quality rugby which they found difficult to handle.*

To sum up, what has been your view of the tour as a whole?

■ *I think the tour has been superb for the country and for New Zealand rugby. The Lions supporters have been magnificent. I think they've enjoyed themselves and their support has been outstanding. They'll be a bit disappointed in the rugby contest, I guess, but the experience of having them here in such great numbers bodes well for the future. I think it proves that we are capable of staging the 2011 Rugby World Cup.*

BELOW A rivalry ends? Graham Henry and Sir Clive Woodward shake hands after the third Test.

Postscript ■ Colin Meads

The following piece, giving the verdict of All Black legend Colin Meads, was edited by Ian Robertson from a BBC interview:

What was your reaction to the news that the Lions squad would be 45 strong on the playing side with almost 30 in the coaching and management team?

■ *I could see the argument for taking more than the squad of 30 which they used to take in my playing days in the 1960s and early 70s but 45 seemed too many for such a short tour. The problem was the selection of four hookers, four half backs and four first five-eighths which meant that by the time they had played each of these players in one of the first four matches the first Test was almost upon them. The Test team never had any chance to play together let alone blend before that opening Test. It seemed very strange that so many of that Christchurch Test team had only started in one match out of the first six. Players like Jonny Wilkinson, Stephen Jones, Jason Robinson, Gareth Thomas, Neil Back and Shane Byrne had precious little match practice together before the Test series got under way.*

There was also the danger with so many different coaches from the different countries that it was difficult to build a pattern of play and style that everyone wanted to adopt. In my day we had Fred Allen and we did it his way. Fred Allen would not have wanted ten different coaches to offer him advice and help him but that is exactly what Sir Clive Woodward had. Fred Allen was sole coach and he would not have wanted it any other way.

What was the biggest disappointment about the tour from a Lions point of view?

■ *It was obviously very disappointing that they lost Lawrence Dallaglio in the very first game of the tour and then that they lost Brian O'Driscoll and Richard Hill early in the first Test. Unlike the losing tours in 1966, 1977, 1983 and 1993 no great stars hit top form in the Test series. There was no Lions player in any of the three Test matches in 2005 who had an outstanding game or who even produced a really memorable 40 minutes. That was not the case in those earlier losing tours.*

The main problem was that the first Test team was picked on reputation not on current form and it was no surprise that they were so completely outplayed by the All Blacks. That meant that to have any chance in the rest of the series they had to start all over again with 11 changes for the second Test and they never recovered from the very disappointing team selection for that disastrous first Test.

The Lions weren't very convincing in the various victories in the provincial matches, were they?

■ *They won them all apart from the Maori match but they were not up against the strongest provinces and it has to be said that none of the 2005 All Blacks were involved in these games. In the old days the All Blacks always played in the provincial games and that would have given the Lions a much better challenge. In most cases a lot of the Super 12 players were also missing so the Lions were not fully tested.*

What about the All Blacks – just how good a side is this?

■ *They certainly won the Test series very convincingly. You can't argue with a scoreline total from the three Tests of 107 points to 40. The try count was pretty one-sided too – the All Blacks scored 12 tries, the Lions only 3.*

Also in terms of individual stars the Lions produced none in the Tests; the All Blacks had several. Notably Dan Carter, Tana Umaga and Sitiveni Sivivatu in the backs, as well as both scrum halves – Byron Kelleher and Justin Marshall. In the pack Richie McCaw was brilliant in the two Tests he played, and his loose-forward colleagues Rodney So'oialo and Jerry Collins were not far behind, but the best of all throughout the series was lock Chris Jack.

My feeling is that there is huge potential in this side and they are already a very good team. After a really good display in the first Test in Christchurch, they were quite

FACING PAGE All Black flanker Jerry Collins is beaten to the ball this time by Simon Easterby but was a star of the series alongside Rodney So'oialo (No. 7) and Richie McCaw, absent injured here in Auckland and replaced by Sione Lauaki (No. 8).

outstanding in the second Test . I don't suppose that Wilkinson has ever been so comprehensively outplayed at international level as he was by 23-year-old Daniel Carter.

The All Blacks were pretty good in the first half of the third Test in Auckland and they had the game won by half-time with a lead of 24–12. They then played their worst 40 minutes of the series but still managed to outscore the Lions by two tries to one.

The three coaches, Graham Henry, Steve Hansen and Wayne Smith, have done a good job in bringing this team on, but they are not yet the finished article. They are a young side with enormous potential …

By the end of November, after the Tri-Nations and their four Tests against the four Home Unions, we will know if they are a great All Black side. The signs are very encouraging.

JVC Flat TV

32" 16:9 LCD TV with Integrated Digital TV Receiver (IDTV)
High resolution W-XGA (1366 X 768) Panel
with Dynamic Black level Picture and Text Dual Screen
3D Sound. Supplied with Table Top stand

• IDTV (Integrated Digital TV Receiver) • W-XGA (1366 x 768) panel • D.I.S.T. (Digital Image Scaling Technology) for High-resolution Picture • Core components: High precision I-P Converter and Formatter • Supporting components: Super DigiPure, IC with dedicated 32-bit CPU to process Dynamic Picture Management, Colour Management, Dynamic Black Level Control and Gamma Curve Control • 20W Total RMS Output • Capability to receive HD 1080i 50/60Hz and HD 720p 60Hz signals • 1-tuner PAP (Picture-and-Picture) • 12 Multi picture • Picture and Text Dual Screen • Front 2 Oblique Cone speakers • 3D Sound • AHB (Active Hyper Bass) • BBE(R) Sound System • Component input • PC Input • 2 SCARTs • S-In, AV-In • Supplied with tabletop stand

DynaPIX   InteriArt   **IDTV**   **BBE**   31-pin-ACART   3D Sound   Picture and Text   **D.I.S.T.**   SCALING   PC In

LT-32D50 DYNAPIX LCD IDTV WITH D.I.S.T

Ranges

17   23   26   32

JVC
The Perfect Experience

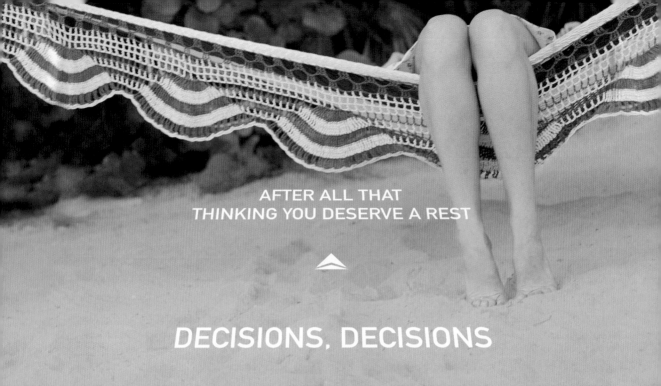

AFTER ALL THAT
THINKING YOU DESERVE A REST

DECISIONS, DECISIONS

CALIFORNIA?
THE CARIBBEAN? CHILE?

delta.com/uk

Delta offers daily non-stop flights from London and Manchester to the U.S., with convenient connections to over 170 destinations throughout the U.S., Latin America and the Caribbean.

For further information please call 0800 414 767 or visit our website.

Saturday 4 June Rotorua International Stadium
Bay of Plenty 20 British & Irish Lions 34
(HALF-TIME 17–17)

Bay of Plenty: A Cashmore; F Bolavucu, A Bunting, G McQuoid, A Tahana; M Williams, K Senio; S Davison, A Lutui, M Sorenson; B Upton, W Ormond (c); N Latu, C Bourke, B Castle
Replacements: W Smith for Bourke 45; A Stewart for Bolavucu 50; P Tupao for Sorenson 63; T Filise for Davison 64
Scorers: Tries – Bourke, Williams; Conversions – Williams (2); Penalties – Williams (2)

British & Irish Lions: J Lewsey; M Cueto, B O'Driscoll (c), G Henson, T Shanklin; R O'Gara, D Peel; G Jenkins, G Bulloch, M Stevens; P O'Connell, B Kay; R Hill, M Williams, L Dallaglio
Replacements: M Corry for Dallaglio 21; A Sheridan for Stevens 67; S Thompson for Bulloch 67; G D'Arcy for Henson 70; M Dawson for Shanklin 73
Scorers: Tries – Lewsey (2), Cueto, Shanklin, Peel, D'Arcy; Conversions – O'Gara (2)

Referee Paul Honiss (New Zealand)
Attendance 33,000

Wednesday 8 June Yarrow Stadium, New Plymouth
Taranaki 14 British & Irish Lions 36
(HALF-TIME 7–6)

Taranaki: S Ireland; S Tagicakibau, M Stewart, C Woods, L Mafi; S Young, C Fevre; T Penn, A Hore, G Slater; J Willis, P Tito (c); S Breman, C Masoe, T Soqeta

Replacements: B Watt for Ireland 16; M Harvey for Tagicakibau 40; R Bryant for Soqeta 65; J Eaton for Breman 65; J King for Fevre 69
Scorers: Tries – Masoe, Watt; Conversions – Young (2)

British & Irish Lions: G Murphy; S Horgan, W Greenwood, O Smith, D Hickie; C Hodgson, C Cusiter; G Rowntree, A Titterell, J Hayes; D O'Callaghan, D Grewcock; M Corry (c), L Moody, M Owen
Replacements: G Jenkins for Hayes 48; S Byrne for Titterell 72; G Cooper for Cusiter 75
Scorers: Tries – Corry, Horgan, Murphy (2); Conversions – Hodgson (2); Penalties – Hodgson (4)

Referee Kelvin Deaker (New Zealand)
Attendance 21,000

Saturday 11 June Waikato Stadium, Hamilton
New Zealand Maori 19 British & Irish Lions 13
(HALF-TIME 6–6)

New Zealand Maori: L MacDonald; R Gear, R Tipoki, L McAlister, C Ralph; D Hill, P Weepu; D Manu, C Flynn, C Hayman; R Filipo, S Hohneck; J Gibbes (c), M Holah, A MacDonald
Replacements: C Spencer for Hill 42; G Feek for Manu 53; D Braid for Filipo 62
Scorers: Try – MacDonald; Conversion – McAlister; Penalties – Hill (2), McAlister (2)

British & Irish Lions: J Lewsey; T Shanklin, B O'Driscoll (c), G D'Arcy, S Williams; S Jones, M Dawson; A Sheridan, S Thompson, J White; S Shaw, P O'Connell; R Hill, M Williams, M Owen

Replacements: S Byrne for Thompson 72;
G Jenkins for Sheridan 48
Scorers: Try – O'Driscoll; Conversion – Jones;
Penalties – Jones (2)

Referee Steve Walsh (New Zealand)
Attendance 30,000

Wednesday 15 June Westpac Stadium, Wellington
Wellington 6 British & Irish Lions 23
(HALF-TIME 6–13)

Wellington: S Paku; L Fa'atau, M Nonu,
T Tu'ipulotu, R Kinikinilau; J Gopperth, P Weepu;
J McDonnell (c), M Schwalger, T Fairbrother;
L Andrews, R Filipo; K Ormsby, B Herring,
T Waldrom
Replacements: K Thompson for Herring 40;
L Mahoney for Schwalger 58; C Jane for Kinikinilau
68; J Purdie for Filipo 71; R Flutey for Weepu 74
Scorers: Penalties – Gopperth (2)

British & Irish Lions: J Lewsey; J Robinson,
B O'Driscoll (c), G Henson, G Thomas; J
Wilkinson, D Peel; G Jenkins, S Byrne, J White;
D Grewcock, B Kay; S Easterby, N Back, M Corry
Replacements: S Jones for Henson 62;
S Horgan for Lewsey 68; C Cusiter for Peel 73;
M Stevens for White 73
Scorers: Tries – Jenkins, Thomas; Conversions –
Wilkinson (2); Penalties – Wilkinson (3)

Referee Paul Honiss (New Zealand)
Attendance 39,000

Saturday 18 June Carisbrook, Dunedin
Otago 19 British & Irish Lions 30
(HALF-TIME 13–13)

Otago: G Horton; H Pedersen, N Brew,
S Mapusua, M Saunders; N Evans, D Lee;
C Dunlea, J MacDonald, C Hoeft; T Donnelly,
F Levi; G Webb, J Blackie, C Newby (c)
Replacements: J Shoemark for Brew 47;
J Smylie for Dunlea 50; J Vercoe for MacDonald
73; C Smylie for Lee 76
Scorers: Try – Lee; Conversion – Evans;
Penalties – Evans (4)

British & Irish Lions: G Murphy; D Hickie,
W Greenwood, G D'Arcy, S Williams; C Hodgson,
C Cusiter; G Rowntree, G Bulloch (c), M Stevens;
S Shaw, D O'Callaghan; S Easterby, M Williams,
R Jones
Replacements: O Smith for D'Arcy 48;
M Dawson for Cusiter 61; D Grewcock for Shaw
61; S Thompson for Bulloch 61; A Sheridan for
Rowntree 61; R O'Gara for Hodgson 70; M Owen
for Jones 76
Scorers: Tries – Greenwood, Jones, S Williams;
Conversions – Hodgson (3); Penalties – Hodgson (3)

Referee Lyndon Bray (New Zealand)
Attendance 26,000

Tuesday 21 June Rugby Park Stadium, Invercargill
Southland 16 British & Irish Lions 26
(HALF-TIME 3–10)

Southland: J Wilson; M Harrison, B Milne,
F Muliaina, W Lotawa; R Apanui, J Cowan;
P Miller, H T-Pole, H Tamariki; D Quate,
H Macdonald; A Dempsey, J Rutledge,
C Dermody (c)
Replacements: J Wright for Miller 38; J Murch
for Dempsey 51; D Hall for Rutledge 57;
P Te Whare for Milne 59; R Logan for Quate 76;
A Clarke for Cowan 79
Scorers: Try – T-Pole; Conversion – Apanui;
Penalties – Apanui (3)

British & Irish Lions: G Murphy; M Cueto, O Smith, G Henson, D Hickie; R O'Gara, G Cooper; M Stevens, A Titterell, J Hayes; S Shaw, D O'Callaghan; L Moody, M Williams, M Owen (c)
Replacements: A Sheridan for Stevens 40; T Shanklin for Smith 48; G Bulloch for Titterrell 48; C Cusiter for Cooper 49; S Easterby for Owen 65; G D'Arcy for Murphy 76
Scorers: Tries – Henson (2); Conversions – O'Gara (2); Penalties – O'Gara (4)

Referee Kelvin Deaker (New Zealand)
Attendance 17,000

Saturday 25 June Jade Stadium, Christchurch
New Zealand 21 British & Irish Lions 3
(HALF-TIME 11–0)

New Zealand: L MacDonald; D Howlett, T Umaga (c), A Mauger, S Sivivatu; D Carter, J Marshall; T Woodcock, K Mealamu, C Hayman; C Jack, A Williams; J Collins, R McCaw, R So'oialo
Replacements: B Kelleher for Marshall 67; G Somerville for Woodcock 67; M Muliaina for MacDonald 69; R Gear for Umaga 75; D Witcombe for Mealamu 75; S Lauaki for Collins 77
Scorers: Tries – Williams, Sivivatu; Conversion – Carter; Penalties – Carter (3)

British & Irish Lions: J Robinson; J Lewsey, B O'Driscoll (c), J Wilkinson, G Thomas; S Jones, D Peel; G Jenkins, S Byrne, J White; P O'Connell, B Kay; R Hill, N Back, M Corry
Replacements: W Greenwood for O'Driscoll 2; R Jones for Hill 18; S Horgan for Robinson 57; D Grewcock for Kay 57; S Thompson for Byrne 57; M Dawson for Peel 74
Scorers: Penalty – Wilkinson
Referee Joel Jutge (France)
Attendance 37,200

Tuesday 28 June Arena Manawatu, Palmerston North
Manawatu 6 British & Irish Lions 109
(HALF-TIME 6–38)

Manawatu: F Bryant; B Gray, J Campbell, M Oldridge, J Leota; G Smith, J Hargreaves; S Moore, N Kemp (c), K Barrett; T Faleafaga, P Rodgers; H Triggs, J Bradnock, B Matenga
Replacements: B Trew for Smith 48; P Maisiri for Matenga 50; C Moke for Triggs 50; N Buckley for Oldridge 53; I Cook for Barrett 64; D Palu for Hargreaves 72; S Easton for Bradnock 76
Scorers: Penalties – Hargreaves (2)

British & Irish Lions: G Murphy; J Robinson, O Smith, G D'Arcy, S Williams; C Hodgson, C Cusiter; A Sheridan, G Bulloch (c), J Hayes; S Shaw, D O'Callaghan; M Corry, M Williams, M Owen
Replacements: N Back for M Williams 41; B Cockbain for O'Callaghan 41; G Cooper for Cusiter 41; A Titterrell for Bulloch 41; R O'Gara for Hodgson 50; M Cueto for Robinson 52; M Stevens for Hayes 60
Scorers: Tries – S Williams (5), Corry, Murphy, Robinson, Hodgson, Smith, Back, D'Arcy, O'Gara (2), Cueto (2), Cooper; Conversions – Hodgson (7), O'Gara (5)

Referee Lyndon Bray (New Zealand)
Attendance 13,000

Saturday 2nd July Westpac Stadium, Wellington
New Zealand 48 British & Irish Lions 18
(HALF-TIME 21–13)

New Zealand: M Muliaina; R Gear, T Umaga (c), A Mauger, S Sivivatu; D Carter, B Kelleher; T Woodcock, K Mealamu, G Somerville; C Jack, A Williams; J Collins, R McCaw, R So'oialo

Replacements: L MacDonald for Mauger 38; J Marshall for Kelleher 66; S Lauaki for Collins 66; D Witcombe for Mealamu 70; M Nonu for Sivivatu 73; J Gibbes for Jack 74; C Johnstone for Woodcock 78
Scorers: Tries – Umaga, Sivivatu, Carter (2), McCaw; Conversions – Carter (4); Penalties Carter (5)

British & Irish Lions: J Lewsey; J Robinson, G Thomas (c), G Henson, S Williams; J Wilkinson, D Peel; G Jenkins, S Thompson, J White; P O'Connell, D O'Callaghan; S Easterby, L Moody, R Jones
Replacements: S Horgan for Henson 70; S Jones for Wilkinson 60; G Rowntree for Jenkins 60; M Corry for O'Callaghan 73; S Byrne for Thompson 78
Scorers: Tries – Thomas, Easterby; Conversion – Wilkinson; Penalties – Wilkinson (2)

Referee Andrew Cole (Australia)
Attendance 39,000

Tuesday 5 July Eden Park, Auckland
Auckland 13 British & Irish Lions 17
(HALF-TIME 3–14)

Auckland: B Ward; I Nacewa, B Atiga, S Tuitupou, J Rokocoko; T Lavea, S Devine; S Taumoepeau, S Telefoni, J Afoa; B Mika, B Williams, J Collins (c), D Braid, A MacDonald
Replacements: J Kaino for Mika 45; C Heard for Taumoepeau 62; K Haiu for MacDonald 67; G Williams for Nacewa 70; J Fonokalafi for Telefoni 76; I Toe'ava for Ward 76
Scorers: Try – Nacewa; Conversion – Ward; Penalties – Ward (2)

British & Irish Lions: G Murphy; M Cueto, W Greenwood, G D'Arcy, D Hickie; C Hodgson,

M Dawson; G Rowntree, G Bulloch (c), J Hayes; S Shaw, B Kay; Jason White, M Williams, M Owen
Replacements: R O'Gara for Hodgson 21; B Cockbain for Kay 35; S Horgan for Greenwood 49; M Corry for White 54; M Stevens for Hayes 59
Scorers: Try – Williams; Penalties – Hodgson, O'Gara (3)

Referee Steve Walsh (New Zealand)
Attendance 45,000

Saturday 9 July Eden Park, Auckland
New Zealand 38 British & Irish Lions 19
(HALF-TIME 24–12)

New Zealand: M Muliaina; R Gear, T Umaga (c), C Smith, S Sivivatu; L McAlister, B Kelleher; T Woodcock, K Mealamu, G Somerville; C Jack, A Williams; J Collins, R So'oialo, S Lauaki
Replacements: M Holah for Lauaki 40; C Johnstone for Woodcock 45; J Marshall for Kelleher 47; J Ryan for Jack 77
Scorers: Tries – Smith, Umaga (2), Williams, Gear; Conversions – McAlister (5); Penalty – McAlister

British & Irish Lions: G Murphy; J Lewsey, W Greenwood, G Thomas (c), M Cueto; S Jones, D Peel; G Jenkins, S Byrne, J White; P O'Connell, D O'Callaghan; S Easterby, L Moody, R Jones
Replacements: G Rowntree for Jenkins 49; M Dawson for Peel 49; S Horgan for Thomas 51; R O'Gara for Murphy 65; G Bulloch for Byrne 70; M Corry for O'Callaghan 73; M Williams for Moody 78
Scorers: Try – Moody; Conversion – S Jones; Penalties – S Jones (4)

Referee Jonathan Kaplan (South Africa)
Attendance 39,000

Tour summary

Name	All matches	Tests
Neil Back	2 + 1	1
Gordon Bulloch	4 + 2	0 + 1
Shane Byrne	3 + 3	2 + 1
Brent Cockbain	0 + 2	
Gareth Cooper	1 + 2	
Martin Corry	4 + 4	1 + 2
Mark Cueto	4 + 1	1
Chris Cusiter	3 + 2	
Gordon D'Arcy	4 + 2	
Lawrence Dallaglio	1	
Matt Dawson	2 + 4	0 + 2
Simon Easterby	4 + 1	2
Will Greenwood	4 + 1	1 + 1
Danny Grewcock	2 + 2	0 + 1
John Hayes	4	
Gavin Henson	4	1
Denis Hickie	4	
Richard Hill	3	1
Charlie Hodgson	4	
Shane Horgan	1 + 5	0 + 3
Gethin Jenkins	5 + 2	3
Ryan Jones	3 + 1	2 + 1
Stephen Jones	3 + 2	2 + 1
Ben Kay	4	1
Josh Lewsey	6	3
Lewis Moody	4	2

Name	All matches	Tests
Geordan Murphy	6	1
Donncha O'Callaghan	6	2
Paul O'Connell	5	3
Brian O'Driscoll	4	1
Ronan O'Gara	2 + 4	0 + 1
Malcolm O'Kelly		
Michael Owen	5 + 1	
Dwayne Peel	5	3
Jason Robinson	4	2
Graham Rowntree	3 + 2	0 + 2
Tom Shanklin	2 + 1	
Simon Shaw	5	
Andrew Sheridan	2 + 3	
Ollie Smith	3 + 1	
Matt Stevens	3 + 3	
Simon Taylor		
Gareth Thomas	4	3
Steve Thompson	2 + 3	1 + 1
Andy Titterrell	2 + 1	
Jason White	1	
Julian White	5	3
Jonny Wilkinson	3	2
Martyn Williams	6 + 1	0 + 1
Shane Williams	4	1

(STARTS + REPLACEMENT APPEARANCES)

Tries

6 S Williams

3 M Cueto, G Murphy

2 M Corry, G D'Arcy, G Henson, J Lewsey, R O'Gara, G Thomas

1 N Back, G Cooper, S Easterby, W Greenwood, C Hodgson, S Horgan, G Jenkins, R Jones, L Moody, B O'Driscoll, D Peel, J Robinson, T Shanklin, O Smith, M Williams

Kickers

	Penalties	Conversions	Points
C Hodgson	8	12	48
R O'Gara	7	9	39
J Wilkinson	6	3	24
S Jones	6	2	22

IT'S NOT JUST ON THE PITCH THAT THE ALL BLACKS LIKE THEIR PERSONAL SPACE

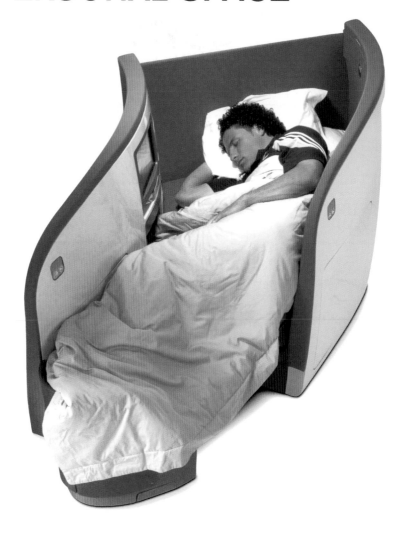

Rugby is always a great reason to visit New Zealand but it's not the only one. With the choice of three new cabins, one of the world's best lie-flat business seats, personal on demand digital entertainment systems, friendly Kiwi hospitality and the feeling of freedom, relaxation and personal space on Air New Zealand will make your journey fly by like a dream. Visit our website and find out more about our exciting on-board transformation.

ALL BLACKS®

AIR NEW ZEALAND

A STAR ALLIANCE MEMBER

Bringing New Zealand close